WINCHESTER

AN ARCHITECT'S VIEW

WINCHESTER
AN ARCHITECT'S VIEW

Peter Kilby

WITPRESS

Published by

WIT Press
Ashurst Lodge, Ashurst, Southampton, SO40 7AA, UK
Tel: 44 (0) 238 029 3223; Fax: 44 (0) 238 029 2853
E-Mail: witpress@witpress.com
http://www.witpress.com

For USA, Canada and Mexico

Computational Mechanics Inc
25 Bridge Street, Billerica, MA 01821, USA
Tel: 978 667 5841; Fax: 978 667 7582
E-Mail: info@compmech.com
US site: http://www.compmech.com

British Library Cataloguing-in-Publication Data

A Catalogue record for this book is available
from the British Library

ISBN: 1-85312-584-9
ISSN: 1466-7258

Library of Congress Catalog Card Number: 99-68719

CONTENTS

ACKNOWLEDGEMENTS

Thanks are due to David R Taylor, ARPS of Headbourne Worthy, Winchester for the following photographs which appear in this book.

FOREWORD

Each generation writes its own history - in effect it constructs a view of the past that is particularly relevant to its own context, intentions and mode of beholding. Peter Kilby takes on the role of interpreter and gives us an architectural perspective.

Winchester is one of the medieval cities on the Pilgrims' Way. It not only rivals Salisbury and Chichester but surpasses them in so many respects - like them, it is multi-layered in its cultural and historical depth: Roman overlays Iron Age, Medieval over Norman, Renaissance over Medieval with substantial 19th and now 20th century interventions.

With a heritage that includes a Cathedral with the longest medieval nave; the Great Hall; St. Cross Hospital; Winchester College; fragments, and certainly the memory, of a palace by Christopher Wren which resides in the Barracks and was intended to rival Versailles, here is material, myth and legend enough to promote popular as well as scholastic interest. One would anticipate historians or archaeologists exploring and indulging for us the richness of this legacy as they have in the past. An architect offers a different and welcome view – an emphasis not only on the history but how this connects to the contemporary scene and the promise of Winchester to come. Peter Kilby exploits this opportunity with new revelations, illustrations and insights into a previously unfocussed 19th and 20th century experience. Nineteenth century architects such as Butterfield, Owen Brown Carter, Blomfield and Baker come under his scrutiny, adding a width of interest to Winchester's historical treasures.

Fashionable interest in urban morphology make Winchester exceptional with its Roman orthoganal layout, in contrast to the usual medieval radial-centric layout. The enclosing wall within a wall, precinct within precinct wets the appetite of any urban designer and gives a reassuring awareness of our need for security that represents a privilege but not exclusion.

This is a timely historical reading for a city that needs the architectural confidence to embark on the many challenges that will confront it in the 21st century.

Professor Sir Colin Stansfield Smith

PROLOGUE

During the late 1990's I was commissioned to write this book, as a sequel to my previous publication by WIT Press, entitled "Southampton Through The Ages". The main manuscript was completed for the present volume in 2001, although there has been a further gestation period during which the photography has been completed and original illustrations and artwork assembled. Armed with my 20 years old Pentax SP 1000 camera, and more recently with a Canon IXUS L-1, the gathering of the information has been systematically carried out, travelling around mainly on foot, exploring the inner workings of this fascinating and historic city. Along the way I have been ably assisted and encouraged by David Taylor ARPS, who has dealt with much of the specialist photography, and which has been formally acknowledged later in this book.

Many kind individuals and organisations have afforded much help, and it is my pleasure to record here the various contributions made, in the preparation of this book.

In Chapters 1 and 10, permission was granted by the Dean and Chapter of the Cathedral, for permission to take the interior photographs, and to reproduce copies of archive drawings of the 1905-12 repairs, drawn by the then Cathedral Architect, Sir Thomas Jackson. The Cathedral Curator, John Hardacre gave much assistance, in sourcing this material. Permission is acknowledged for access to No. 10 The Close; to photograph the stunning 13th Century vaulted room, in the home of the Cathedral Director of Music.

Much of the original research has been carried out in the Hampshire Record Office, and my appreciation of the help and assistance from the staff there cannot be overstated. Similarly in the Hampshire Local Studies Collection, County Library, help was always at hand. In Chapter 4 permission was given on behalf of Hampshire County Council, by Kerrie Harris Principal Administration Officer, to take photographs of The Great Hall.

The Photographs in Chapter 5, were taken by kind permission of the Warden and Fellows of Winchester College, the arrangements for which were made by Mr J.J Brecknell, Assistant Bursar, and Mr Sid Skinner (late of the "Met"), who guided me around the College Buildings.

Access to The Hospital of St. Cross and Almshouse of Noble Poverty was arranged by the Hospital Administrator Miriam Phillips, and permission was granted on behalf of The Master and Trustees to take photographs inside the grounds and buildings open to the public of this venerable institution. (Now reproduced in Chapter 6).

The visits to the many City Churches has been assisted by both incumbents and church officials, including the Rector of St. Lawrence Church, the Rev. D.V. Scott, the management of Debenhams Department

Store, for giving access to the Bell Tower of the Church of St. Maurice from the Cathedral View Restaurant, the Officials of the Chesil Theatre for permission to visit the inside of St. Peter's Chesil, (now a theatre), and to Mr B. Poole for his notes on St. Paul's Church and introduction to the existence there of the exiting murals by Heywood Sumner.

In Chapter 9 access to the various Victorian institutions was gained and granted as follows. Permission to take photographs within the Chapel of Royal Hampshire County Hospital, by the architect William Butterfield was arranged by Miss Wendy Turner the Trust Administrator, who kindly presented me with a copy of Barbara Turner's " History of the Royal Hampshire County Hospital". I am indebted to the Governor of H.M. Prison Winchester for permission to visit the prison and also to Sue Shuttlewood Personel EO for showing me around this impressive edifice dating from Victorian times, which produced a thought provoking experience. Thanks also to Chris Higgins, Director of Estates at King Alfred's College, for providing a copy of the 1862 Engraving of the then "Diocesan Training College", and for allowing me to see the college buildings within the campus. The Rev T. Dakin, now Vicar of St. Mary's Fordingbridge, (Past Chaplain of King Alfred's College), gave invaluable assistance with background information as to the history of the college. Permission was granted to visit the buildings of the Hospital of St. John and its Chapel and to take photographs.

In Chapter 10, I am indebted to Celia Green, the Secretary at the Wessex Hotel, for showing me record photographs of the excavations carried out before the hotel was built on the old Cathedral carpark and for background information on the William Walker Restaurant opened there in 1998.

Additionally, I wish to thank Michael Morris for reading the manuscript and making many helpful and pertinent comments, and Sir Colin Stansfield for his patient advice and agreeing to write the Foreword to the book, which is very much appreciated.

Finally, there are thanks to be made of a more personal nature, about people who have helped sustain the long effort in writing this book. Firstly to my wife Alice for her horticultural input to the "Open Spaces" of Chapter 7 and for the countless tea and coffee breaks. Next, I would like to thank Anne Mitchell, my near neighbour in Fordingbridge, for teaching me to manipulate the intricacies of my computer to produce a copy of the manuscript for my publishers. Thanks also to WIT Press and in particular to Keith Godwin for the excellent and imaginative graphic design, to Brian Privett for his patience with my temperament, and to Lance Sucharov my Publishing Director, and to Professor Carlos Brebbia who asked me to write this book in the first place.

Peter Kilby
Author

*This book is dedicated to
all my family and to the
memory of my parents.*

St. Catherine's Hill

A single rampart and ditch defended this Iron Age Hillfort of some 9.3 hectares, with its entrance on the north-east. Dating from circa 3BC, it was essentially both a stronghold and market- place until it was abandoned around 1BC. The ridge is marked by a clump of trees, signifying the location of a lost early medieval chapel dedicated to St. Catherine, martyred and tortured on a spiked wheel, hence the term "catherine- wheel".

Chapter 1

AN HISTORICAL INTRODUCTION

Winchester as we know it today was founded in Roman times in about the year A.D.70, quite soon in fact after Roman legions landed downstream on the east bank of the River Itchen in A.D.43, and set up their camp at Clausentum (the earlier settlement at Southampton), some 12 miles to the south. There were of course previous settlements around such as the Iron Age Fort on St. Catherine's Hill to the south-east of Winchester, but this was abandoned in about 100 B.C. It was at this time that a new settlement on lower ground at Oram's Arbour of about 20 hectares came into being, just on the north west corner of the subsequent Roman Winchester, but this also closed down in about 50 B.C. The establishment of Winchester or **Venta Belgarum** by the Romans created a town of truly urban proportions, in an area of hitherto scattered homesteads and small settlements.

Geographically Winchester stands in the main on the west side of the River Itchen, and its gridded street pattern and regular shape, within the original enclosing walls, is orientated on a south-westerly axis in line with the prevailing south-westerly winds. It is quite clear that the Romans carefully chose this site, and amended its shape to accommodate a new town by diverting the main stream of the River Itchen to the east and flattening part of the Oram's Arbour complex to the north-west to incorporate some of its land into the chosen site. This new town encompassed an area of about 58.2 hectares and was protected by a wall, a section of which can still be seen in a recess near the old City Bridge. Within the curtilage of the enclosing walls, and over the centuries of the Roman occupation, there developed a highly organised, educated and civilised society, supported by a sophisticated infrastructure of piped water supply, mains drainage and heated installations such as bath houses.

The Roman occupation lasted some 300 years or so when in A.D.410 Emperor Honorius put an end to the control over "Britannia" from the central government in Rome, after which the structure of the imported civilisation ebbed away, the financial system collapsed and with it trade and prosperity. With the withdrawal of the Roman legions, a social malaise and decline set in and the town with its fortifications, streets and buildings became, in part at least, abandoned.

Today the chief remains of this occupation, apart from the street pattern, (which was subsequently changed centuries later in Saxon times), are the cemeteries now hidden from view but nevertheless extant outside the lines of the Roman walls. These cemeteries formed the necropolis or **"The City of the Dead"** and conformed to Roman law by siting burials outside the City, to prevent both physical contamination of the drinking water supply, as well as protecting the spirituality of the living world. Some 675 burials have been excavated with the graves cut into the chalk and set out in lines, with heads facing to the west, and in some instances containing so-called "grave goods" for the journey into the after-life. These burials give

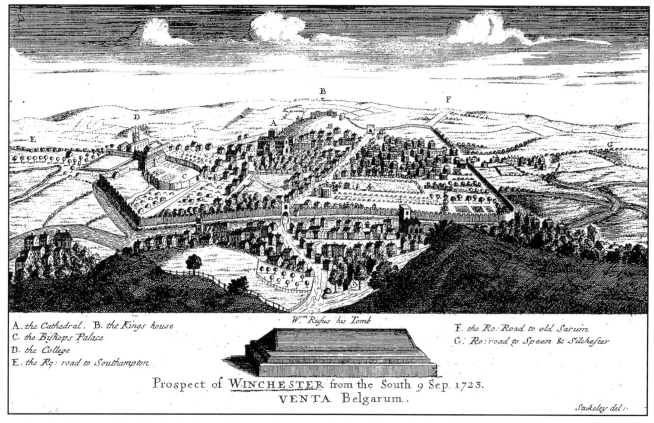

A. the Cathedral. B. the Kings house
C. the Bishops Palace
D. the College
E. the Rd: road to Southampton

Wm Rufus his Tomb

F. the Ro: Road to old Sarum
G. Ro:road to Speen & Silchester

Prospect of WINCHESTER from the South 9 Sep. 1723.
VENTA Belgarum.

Stukeley del:

**Engraving of 1723 by Stukeley, of Venta Belgarum,
the Roman name for Winchester.**
*The Cathedral, The King's House, The Bishop's Palace, and
Winchester College, all feature here. In addition the Roman
Roads to Southampton, Sarum, (Salisbury), and Silchester are all
noted. (Reproduced by courtesy of the Hampshire Record Office).*

insight into the rigours of life 2000 years ago with infant mortality rife and life expectancy of adults only 20-30 years! Some additional evidence of the reason for the surprisingly short life expectancy, in spite of the civilising facilities available at the time, is revealed by the high lead content found in the bones of skeletons, probably as the result of drinking water transmitted through lead pipes.

These burials represent tangible evidence, and together with finds of past archaeological excavations, which for instance at **The Brooks** revealed not only Roman street patterns, but also details of both its buildings and way of life, together with examples of great artistry in the form of beautiful mosaic floors dating from the 2nd century A.D., the centrepiece of which is the "flower mosaic" incorporating the emotive swastika motive. These artifacts are the primary sources of the City's Roman History, in that like the only small remaining section of the town wall set against the west bank of the River Itchen, they bear witness to a brilliant and advanced civilisation which has long since passed away, but are a cogent reminder of the influences which are still present today.

After the passing of the Romans the history of Winchester is inextricably linked with the Christian faith, since knowledge of Christianity would have doubtlessly been introduced by default by the Romans themselves and by traders coming to this country from the Middle East. The first entry in the Anglo-Saxon Chronicles which mentions Winchester is for the year A.D. 641, which states *"Cenwalh ordered the church at Winchester to be built; he was the son of Cynegils"(King Cenwalh reigned from A.D. 642-72).* The church referred to would be the "**Old Minster**", being the forerunner together with the "**New Minster**", of the present-day Cathedral. Within the Venerable Bede's "Ecclesiastical History of the English People" he writes *"At that time (i.e. A.D.635), during the reign of Cynegils, the west Saxons, anciently known as the Gewissaw, accepted the faith of Christ through the preaching of Bishop Birinius."* In other words these two sources of Anglo-Saxon history confirm the acceptance of Christianity in Winchester with the erection of an early, if not its earliest, Christian church.

There were, however, dark pagan forces at work in the guise of the **Vikings**, who in their long boats came from Scandinavia to plunder and pillage throughout the country, quite often led by noblemen ousted in their own country, and seeking new lands to conquer and ultimately colonise. In the year A.D. 860, it is recorded in the Anglo-Saxon Chronicles, *"a great ship-force came and destroyed Winchester. Against that force fought eldorman Osric with the men of Hampshire and Aethelwulf with the men of Berkshire. They put the force to flight and had the power of the battlefield."* Although these Vikings were warriors at first they eventually settled and became farmers, but not without taking land by coercion, and it was for this reason that help was to come to hand with the accession of **King Alfred** to the throne of Wessex in A.D. 871.

King Alfred was to reign until his death in A.D. 899 and was the first King to subjugate warring factions, both at home and from abroad, and to be the undisputed ruler of all England; combining the rare qualities of being both a warrior and a man of peace and learning. It was during his kingship that the **Anglo-Saxon Chronicles** flourished in great detail, and although there is no firm evidence that King Alfred ordered the compilation of these Chronicles he certainly acted as their inspiration. Today his memory is honored by the vast warrior statue in The Broadway close to the Guildhall, recording at the same time that he drove the Danish from Wessex, and established the fortified "burhrs" (boroughs) of which Winchester was the capital. In addition to being a scholar he was also a deeply religious man and actively encouraged the establishment of monastic life in this country.

Winchester at the time of King Alfred was fortified, the Roman walls were rebuilt, and within this area a new grid of streets imposed upon the Roman prototype plan. In order to balance the need for defence against the need also to both sow and reap crops and to generally farm the countryside, Alfred devised the clever scheme of *"rotation of service"* which meant that able-bodied men took it in turns between being farmers and soldiers. Alfred is also acknowledged as the founder of the English Navy in that he foresaw the need to combine his landward defence strategy, with defending his coastline from seaward incursions and attack inland. While all these measures were being put into effect, Alfred sought to promote social change from his Winchester headquarters, in that he brought about a survey of the counties, parishes and hundreds of his kingdom, an idea seized upon hundreds of years later by William the Conqueror in the 12th century. Out of this survey Alfred formulated laws, which have been handed down forming the basis of present-day Common Law and social justice.

Reference has already been made to the **"Old Minster"** founded in the year A.D. 641 and completed in A.D. 643, the lines of whose foundations have been located by archaeological excavations and can today be seen at an angle, and immediately adjacent to the north aisles of the present Cathedral. Unlike the Cathedral itself, the Old Minster is orientated east-west in its exactitude, whilst the Cathedral is aligned parallel to the grid of the Roman/Saxon town. Just to the north and immediately adjacent to the remains of the Old Minster is the site of the **"New Minster"** built in A.D. 903, only a metre away, so close in fact that it is said that the sounds of the services in the two churches used to mingle! During the excavations carried out in 1965, within the "Old Minster" part of a narrative frieze was unearthed showing scenes of the Saga of Sigmund and the Wolf, thought to represent the ancestors of Denmark and Wessex, harking back to the burial of King Canute (Cnut) in the "Old Minster" in the year A.D. 1035, and his Viking ancestry.

With the foundation of the **Cathedral Church of St. Mary** in Winchester in 1079, 13 years after the Norman Conquest of 1066, there came with it a tangible manifestation of the ideals of the *"Regularis Concordia"* when earlier in A.D. 975 the then Bishop of Winchester, Aethelwold, set up a new set of monastic regulations that enabled the establishment of Benedictine principles to regulate and control church life which had hitherto been in the hands of lay clergy. The Benedictine monks were enjoined to live an ordered life of prayer, worship and labour, within a preordained community, and at Winchester the evidence of the monastic buildings in which they lived are seen today with the remains of the **Priory of St. Swithun**, established in A.D. 964 and active till the time of the Dissolution of the Monasteries under the orders of King Henry VIII (reigned 1509-47) on the 14th November 1539. At this place, however, in the 10th and 11th centuries there came a high point in monastic life which resulted in the so-called **"Winchester Style"** in the writing and decoration of religious manuscripts, following a return to classical art, upon which English artists improvised with beautiful examples of line drawing and colour to embellish their manuscripts. It is important, therefore, to bear these factors in mind in relation to the Norman Conquest, which merely imposed a new civilisation on one which already existed.

With the coming of the Norman Conquest, castles as opposed to earthwork fortifications were introduced into this country for the first time and Winchester was no exception. In excavations near to the West Gate, we see the remains of the once great edifice of **Winchester Castle;** one of the most powerful fortresses initiated by William the Conqueror. This castle was surrounded by a great barbican ditch with a bridge leading over to the one gatehouse point of entry. The castle was protected by a curtain wall with several towers enclosing the inner bailey with its hall, kitchen, chapel and stables. The most heavily defended area eventually would have been the keep on a mound and protected by a ditch in the southernmost space of the overall enclosure and inter-connected at the northern end with the West Gate and town walls. (The castle was extended and improved over a number of years until besieged by Cromwell's army in the Civil War and demolished afterwards in the year 1651).

Throughout the period of the 12th-14th Centuries, there were several significant events marking the progress of Winchester's history, for example the founding of the **Hospital of St. Cross** by Bishop Henry de Blois in 1137 (being a measure to allay the physical hardship of the time), the modernisation of Winchester Castle in 1222 by Henry III (reigned 1216-72) and the building of the Great Hall. While in 1348 the scourge of the **Black Death** occurred, which in the two years until 1349 killed over one third of the population of England and in Winchester is thought to have accounted for up to half of its population! However, it was during this time that the Romanesque Norman architecture introduced by William the Conqueror's administration, gave way to the flowering of the Early English Gothic style with its pointed arches and slender proportions; a far cry from the seemingly ponderous proportions of Norman design which although at times majestic is nevertheless alien to this land. We see within the confines of **Winchester Cathedral** the total

The King's House from an engraving of 1838, (i.e. before the great fire of 1894). These details coincide with a photograph taken after the fire, of the remains of the buildings then serving as military barracks, being part of the edifices designed by Sir Christopher Wren for King Charles 11 in 1683. New barracks were erected on the same site in 1899. (Reproduced by courtesy of the Hampshire County Council Record Office).

An East View of the KINGS HOUSE at WINCHESTER in HAMPSHIRE. Dedicated to the Officers of the Militia. Engrav'd from a Drawing taken on the Spot by an Officer.

architectural development from Norman style through to Early English and Decorated Gothic and culminating in the so called Perpendicular style; the latter being quintessentially English, having first found expression within Gloucester Cathedral. This architectural expression was able to flourish in company with the power and wealth of the Church in the Middle Ages. Within the Cathedral we see the shrines of the most powerful Bishops culminating in the tomb of **William of Wykeham**, "*most famous of Winchester's sons*" responsible for remodelling the nave of the Cathedral and for founding **Winchester College**.

In the reign of King Henry VIII (1509-47) political unrest and religious changes brought turmoil to Winchester, and throughout the country, with the **Dissolution of the Monasteries** affecting institutions within the town, namely St. Mary's Abbey (1536), Hyde Abbey (1538) and Kingsmill Abbey (1539). Of these three religious centres traces exist today in Hyde Street where the **Hyde Abbey Gateway** remains as a reminder of the Benedictine Nunnery founded in A.D. 965, as the "New Minster" which moved to this site in A.D. 1110. Here, as elsewhere, the monastic buildings were left to decay, forming a blight on substantial areas of the town and at the mercy of those seeking stone for other building projects and repairs. Even the Priory of St. Swithun was not exempt from these outrages, and although attached to a Cathedral Church, the shrine of St. Swithun within the Cathedral itself was destroyed on "order" of the Royal Commissioners in 1538. After these events the sites of all four priories passed to the ownership of Winchester College.

During the period of the **Civil War** the citizens of Winchester were divided in their loyalties, although officially the town was Royalist in its allegiance, as

demonstrated by the sacking of the Cathedral in 1642 by Roundhead troops. It was at this event of sacrilege that elements of decoration within the Cathedral were wantonly smashed by Cromwell's men. Stained glass was the principal target and in the great West Window the fragmented elements of the coloured glass in seemingly abstract patterns, are made up of parts rescued and stored after the sacking. At the same time priceless manuscripts and documents within the Cathedral library were taken and in some cases thrown into the river where the papers floated downstream, some of which arrived at St. Cross where they were rescued by the Brothers. As a final irony there is an apocryphal story concerning the Cathedral itself, where it was noted that the only place which escaped the ravages of destruction was the William of Wykeham Chapel, because it is said that the officer in charge of the operation was himself a Wykehamist!

The same Civil War saw the fall of Winchester Castle to Parliamentary forces in 1645 when the Governor surrendered to Oliver Cromwell and his troops after the walls had been breached by artillery, and by so doing avoided further casualties within the garrison. Subsequently the Castle was demolished in 1651, five years after the war, and it was on this same site that in the 1680's King Charles II (reigned 1649-85) commissioned **Sir Christopher Wren** to design for him a new palace and gardens of considerable splendour, quite out of scale with the rest of the town. The project, however, foundered and was unfinished at the time of the King's death in 1685 and the work which had been completed namely the King's House, was destroyed by fire in 1894 leaving only the Great Hall dating from the 13th century, and the previous edifice in ruins.

Throughout the period of Winchester's history and

The Guildhall from an engraving of 1892
The Guildhall was opened in 1873 and extended in 1892. This charming engraving by C.G.Harper depicts the work under way, behind the main building, during the construction of the banqueting hall. Part of the crenellations of Abbey House, the Mayor's official residence is seen in the foreground.
(Author's Collection).

The Guildhall.

up to, and incorporating the Georgian era, the latter spanning from the reign of George I (reigned 1714-27) to George IV (reigned 1820-30), the town had flourished as a Royal Town. Afterwards, however, the Royal influence was to wane and to be replaced by a new energy with the emergence of trade and the construction of residences for the well-to-do. In addition to this, Winchester had been a military town from 1788 when the militia occupied the King's House, starting a tradition leading through to the present day in the **Peninsula Barracks** on high ground to the north-west of the site of the Castle.

The opening of the **South Western Railway** (formerly the London and Southampton Railway) in May 1840 during the reign of Queen Victoria (1837-1901) linking London Nine Elms to Southampton Terminus, heralded a new era in the mode of transportation for towns along its route including Winchester. In a map dated circa 1850-60, the line of this railway to the west of the parade ground of the Barracks is indicated, with the main station at the north-west corner of the town and a special platform to serve the military site. The main station gave access to all stations between London and Southampton as well as the "Old Docks." By 1848, the final link from Nine Elms (in the parish of Battersea) with Waterloo had been completed. The fastest trains from Southampton made the trip to London in just one hour and fifty minutes! (This should be compared with stagecoach times of ten hours for the same journey).

It was during this era that some notable public buildings emerged in Winchester, for instance the **Royal**

The M3 *and the controversial "cutting" at Twyford Down to the south east of Winchester.*

Hampshire Hospital designed by the eminent Victorian architect William Butterfield in 1854 and opened in 1868. The layout of the wards and treatment rooms were advised upon by Florence Nightingale; best remembered for using statistics to justify her medical theories to a sceptical establishment. (She proved beyond doubt that because of poor non-sterile procedures and unhygienic wards in a war location, men were more likely to die in hospital than on a battlefield!) On the Romsey Road opposite the Hospital, the then **County and City Prison** was completed in 1850,

a monumental edifice when viewed from the higher ground to the north. In The Broadway there is the imposing **Guildhall** built in 1871-3. On the plinth of this building there is a plaque defining its location in exactitude both in relation to its height above sea level (27 feet 2 inches), and its latitude and longitude; while at the same time noting that the time in Winchester is five- sixteenths of a second later than Greenwich!

It was in Victorian times that Winchester became a tourist centre because of good communications afforded by the railway, both in its relationship with London and the port of Southampton to the south, giving direct access to the liners of the passenger trade with worldwide connections. In order to cater for the needs of the visitors, inns and hotels were built providing facilities from which to view at leisure this historic and venerable city. However, there was a downside to all this with a decline in the large town houses when wealthy trades people decided this time to move out to the suburbs. Changes to the infrastructure of the town at that same time resulted in some demolition of the existing redundant buildings, for instance the jail in Jewry Street, following the re-siting of the prison referred to above. The re-organisation of local government was also a live issue at the time with the setting up of the County Council, following the introduction of the Local Government Bill to Parliament in 1888. In 1890 Sir Arthur Blomfield produced designs for the new **County Hall**, to the north of the City's West Gate.

The 20th century began in Winchester by commemorating the millennium of King Alfred's rule with a vast statue erected in The Broadway in 1901 to mark the memory of this warrior king; being a symbol of Winchester's pre-eminence in the history of England. Other landmarks in its history can be recorded such as the restoration of the original foundations of Winchester Cathedral in 1912, as well as the erection of some notable examples of 20th Century architecture. For instance there is the **Wessex Hotel**, built in 1961-3, to the north of the Cathedral, and more recently the **Hampshire Record Office**, a scintillating building in both form and function. Without doubt the most universally publicised event of the 20th century associated with Winchester, must be the saga of the M3 extensions, including the exceptional public meetings and final opposition to this road in the form of demonstrations by the "Dongas", the precursors of the "Eco Warriors", and the impact of their actions on future road building policy in areas of outstanding natural beauty and history.

FOOTNOTE

The purpose of this book is to give an up-to-date picture of the architecture, townscape, and landscape of Winchester set against the social and economic influences of its long history. The primary sources are the buildings themselves, both historic and new, and the narrative which seeks to explain why the city looks the way it does today. The historical introduction sets the scene in broad terms and the chapters which follow describe the most significant areas of the City and its immediate environs irrespective of the chronological content of its buildings, in a way that the reader can trace on foot or also in the imagination.

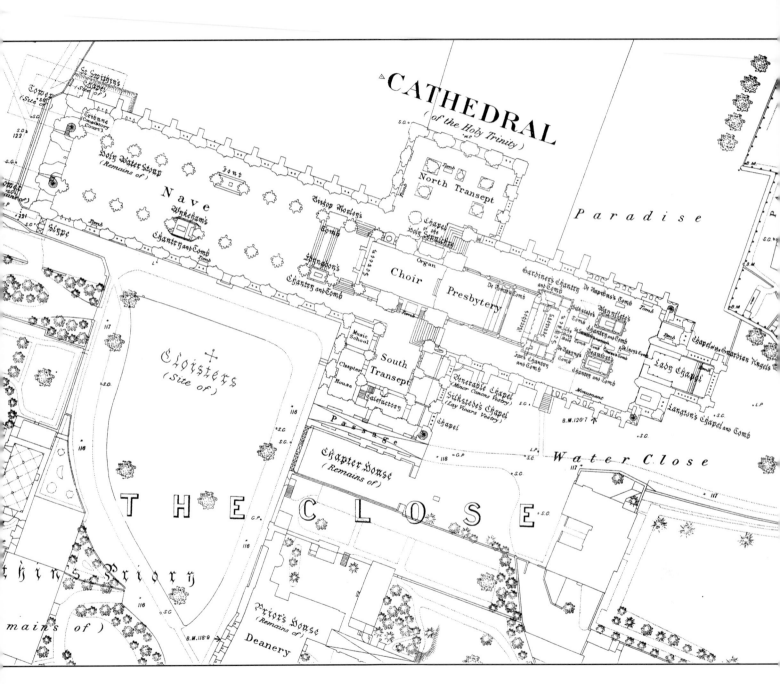

Chapter 2

THE CATHEDRAL PRECINCT AND CLOSE

The Cathedral and Close, lying as they do at the very heart of Winchester, bear witness to the ancient and powerful ecclesiastical foundations within the city, when once the influences both spiritual and political spread out to the very centre of power in this country. The focus of these influences has from Norman times been encapsulated within the present **Cathedral**, dedicated in the 11th century as the **Church of the Holy Trinity**, as well as to the buildings situated to the south namely the **Close** and **Wolvesey Palace** further to the east..

The main entrance to the Close is via the Priory Gate leading from St. Swithun Street, to the south, and immediately adjacent to the Kingsgate, with its triple arched entrance to the city, and above which is the **Church of St. Swithun.** Outside the 15th century Priory Gate, also called St. Swithun's Gate, with its massive stone walls some 2 metres thick, are beautifully carved oak gates under a pointed stone arch, and a wall above finished with crenellations. To the right is the 15th century **Cheyney Court**, (and Porter's Lodge) once used as the Bishop's

The Close, Winchester.

Cheyney Court
Post-Card dated 1904 shows how little has changed over the years notwithstanding its 15th Century origin.
(Author's Collection).

Plan of Winchester Cathedral *(opposite page)*
From an Ordnance Survey Map of 1876.
(Reproduced by courtesy of the Hampshire Local Studies Collection, County Library and the Ordnance Survey.)

The Deanery
This was the Prior's Lodging in medieval times although today it is the official residence of the Dean.

Court House. This is a striking building with triple gables facing the road, (with a fourth gable projecting forward), and attic windows set within the gables. Below at first-floor level is oak half timbering and plaster panels containing two curious projecting bay (oriel) windows, with tiled roofs; and the half timbering itself, encompassing both the gables and the first floor, which form a jetty outwards above the flint and stone ground-floor walls below.

The elevation overall has a somewhat higgledy-piggledy arrangement of windows with one squeezed in to form a fourth level in the **Porter's Lodge**, but the informality adds to its charm. However, recent lime-washes to both timber and plaster have not been colour differentiated to give clarity of architectural expression between the two materials. Nevertheless the building remains photogenically very attractive, nestling against the profusion of the leaves and flowers of the ancient vine which bedecks its façade.

Immediately adjacent, and at right angles to Cheyney Court, is an attractive two storey timber framed building, with dormer windows in the roof, being part of the Pilgrim's School complex, and choir school to the Cathedral. Beyond this, and at the far side of a quadrangle of red brick buildings, is the 14th century **Pilgrims Hall**. Inside this historic edifice is a stone flagged floor, plastered walls and two complete, rough hewn, oak hammer beam roof trusses with carved bosses, thought to be the earliest so far identified in medieval England.

Looking beyond the Pilgrim's School there are some majestic lawns reaching as far as the medieval Deanery with a fine Cedar of Lebanon as a focal landscape feature. The lawns here in **Mirabel Close** are host to a remarkable piece of modern sculpture by Barbara Hepworth, to remind us of the 20th century and impending 21st century, with abstract forms and brilliant colouring. This sculpture, depicting the Crucifixion, first came to view amid some controversy when it appeared in the Close of Salisbury Cathedral. It was sometime later relocated here at Winchester, at least at the time of writing this book. Sculpture in a landscape setting has a poignant and evocative impact. Big sculpture is more at home in the open air, where it can interact with nature, which because of its omnipotent quality does not have any aesthetic preconceptions.

Facing these beautiful lawns is located the **Deanery** which in the Middle Ages was the Prior's Lodging. It is an imposing building facing gable-end-on and built with a

No 9 The Close, i.e. Church House
This elegant 17th Century triple gabled, town house, with its stone façade, is now the home of the Winchester Diocesan Board of Finance and Diocesan Secretary.

The 13th Century vaulted room at 10 The Close
Residence of the Cathedral Musical Director and his Wife, Mr and Mrs David Hill, who kindly gave permission for this photograph to be taken.

semi-basement surmounted by a piano-nobile arrangement containing the 15th century **Prior's Hall.** To the right is a rather diminutive wing, again three storeys but smaller in scale marking the entrance, with a series of three-pointed arches leading to a stone vaulted chamber or porch. Within this porch are some exquisite oak panelled doors under a semi-circular stone arch surmounted by the Gothic vaulting. At right angles and behind there is the interconnected **Long Gallery,** a brick building in contrast to the stonework of the main Deanery buildings. Facing southwards here are fine stone window mullions in the Perpendicular style again of the 15th century, while behind and in the near distance the Cathedral rises into view.

Along the west side of the Deanery are five stone buttresses alongside the Prior's Hall, leading to a brick gable-end surmounted by an extremely tall and elegantly fluted chimney-stack with little semicircular arches set into the face. Beyond this, and to the north, is a great stone

wall with blind arcading, semi-circular Norman arches and columns with seemingly out of place capitals. This is the only tangible reminder of the once great and original **Chapter House** now demolished and lost to posterity. Immediately adjacent to the site of this Chapter House and adjacent also to the south transept of the Cathedral is an arched and vaulted passageway called the **Slype,** which by definition is the name given to the access provision from a cathedral to its chapter house.

Passing through the Slype and on the left the site of the old burial ground for the Priory, referred to in Speed's map of 1611 as "Paradise", **No. 1 The Close** comes into view. This is an imposing brick built house dating from 1699, (now the Winchester Cathedral Office), with two side wings and a central door feature, three storeys in height with dormers in the pitched tiled roof. At first-floor level there are some extremely fine sash windows with half panes on either side, and on the ground floor a stone arched canopy sits majestically above the semi-circular fanlight

Mirabel Close
Barbara Hepworth's 'Construction Crucifixion'. A remarkable piece of modern sculpture, in a timeless landscape setting.

to the six-panelled entrance door. Perhaps the most striking feature of the house is its brickwork which is built in Flemish Bond, (i.e.one brick placed full length and one end on, repeated and staggered), with the end on bricks, called headers, being darker in colour than the ones placed full length named stretchers. This light and dark effect of the red bricks is brought about by the firing process within the kilns, where the bricks are stacked, and the temperature at the top being higher causes the bricks to "burn" there, hence the darker colour. Returning back through the Slype there is a second large lawn, this being on the site of the original Cathedral Cloisters to the south of the Nave, resplendent with soaring buttresses and arches which were part of the 1912 strengthening procedures. Flanking this lawn to the west there is a range of three houses namely **9, 10, and 11 The Close**, quite individual in their respective appearances. **No. 9, Church House** was built early in the 17th century, now houses the Winchester Diocesan Board of Finance. This is a house with triple stone gables and walls with two very tall chimneys set into the steeply sloping tiled roof. There are traditional sash windows on the ground and first floors with stone mullions to the windows on the second floor set into the gables. The stone porch and entrance are arranged to one side, while this asymmetrical arrangement sits well by chance or design, with the diagonally placed Close road outside and to the front. Immediately to the right of Church House and attached thereto is **No. 10 The Close** within which is a 13th century vaulted room, quite spectacular and bedecked with musical instruments of the Cathedral Musical Director. Standing back from the open areas of The Close, and enclosed by a high stone wall, No. 11 can be seen through the arch formed by two stone piers with a wrought iron arch and a lantern, being a five bay house dating from

1727. Further to the south and opposite the Deanery is the late 17th century **Judge's Lodging House** a simple brick edifice, outside of which can be seen the judge's official car and police escort on the days when the Crown Courts at the Castle are in session. Finally, near to No. 4 is a cul-de-sac of houses comprising **Nos. 5-8 The Close,** being part of a sequestered enclave away from the comings and goings of the remainder of The Close, or so it would seem.

On the outside and north face of No. 11 The Close is an inscription cut into a plaque of stonework which reads; *"Have in mind William Walkelin Bishop of Winchester 1070-1098. This stone marks the western limit of the south wall"*, and makes reference to the site of the original Norman west front, now demolished. Originally there were twin towers, which extended several metres beyond the west front of the present Cathedral, following the remodelling of the nave started in 1350 by **Bishop William of Edington** (1345-66) and completed by **Bishop William of Wykeham** (1366-1404). This is a salutary reminder that Winchester

Winchester Cathedral
View of the Cathedral seen from the Wessex Hotel across the Cathedral lawns, with the North Transept and Presbytery nestling beneath the sombre Norman tower.

Cathedral, like many others, and indeed thousands of parish churches up and down the country, has over the centuries assimilated change as part of its evolutionary process. In addition to this, changes have been brought about by the need to repair the fabric over a period of over 900 years; and it is this process which has also been the source of ongoing and continual evolution leading to some parts of the building looking newer than others. The most significant example of this phenomenon is the pristine whiteness of the west front, provoking a first time visitor into thinking that it is "new", but dating in fact from the 14th century!

Let us turn now to the questions of why and how this great Cathedral was built. It has been said that a cathedral combines the dual qualities of both artistic and spiritual expression. Nevertheless to both believers and non-believers alike, there can be no doubting the impact of this Cathedral entered from the west end. It is awesomely impressive. Following the Norman Conquest, **King William** set about sweeping away the finely tuned Saxon culture, taking away the land and money from those who had fought against him at the Battle of Hastings, and at Winchester appointing a Norman Bishop to the Cathedral. Therefore the building, which is evidenced in part at the tower and crossing, symbolises the wealth and power of the State as much as the religious inspiration of the times

Winchester Cathedral - South Transept
This glimpse of the South Transept, with the Slype below, (i.e. the passageway between the Cathedral and the site of the Chapterhouse, now demolished), embodies the essentially Norman origins of the this building..

of its conception.

The building of this great Cathedral began in the year 1079, 13 years after the Norman Conquest of England, and the first stage was completed and dedicated on the 8th April 1093, some 23 years after the appointment of Bishop Walkelin to the Bishopric in 1070. Of this original Norman Cathedral, it is uncertain just how much was finished at that time, but the best guess appears to suggest that the eastern sanctuary, crossing and tower, north and south transepts and several bays of the nave had been completed as well as the crypt. The **crypt** itself being below ground and entered via a stone staircase from the north transept, is historically the oldest part of the building and defines with certainty the east end of the Norman Cathedral, beyond which later additions were to be placed.

The foundations for the Cathedral were set upon timber piles let into the soggy terrain of the Itchen flood plain. The stone used for the building was a grey-white "shelly" limestone from the quarry at **Quarr Abbey** in the Isle of Wight, being transported to the site by sea and probably river, and manhandled to the new Cathedral itself. Bearing in mind the quantity of stone required for this enormous project, as well as the absence of modern machinery for cutting and moving, one can only marvel at the skill and fortitude of the medieval labourers and masons. As for the building operations, both scaffolding and formwork were constructed in timber, a far cry from present-day steel scaffolding, being engineering structures

in their own right. Having said this, when all the phases were finally completed in the late 15th and early 16th centuries, Winchester Cathedral encompassed some 169.5 metres in length measured outside, and is the longest medieval cathedral in this country and possibly Europe.

The main external envelope walls of this great Cathedral being constructed in stone are "par excellence", a compression structure, in that all the loads of the building are transmitted to the foundations without the use of steel-reinforcement, which was unknown in medieval times. For instance the tall stone pinnacles, seen above the buttresses on the north and south faces of the nave, are there as a structural counterweight, directing huge thrusting loads downwards from the roof. These pinnacles are architectural features born of necessity, which give poise and elegance to the external appearance in harmony with the colour, texture and patina of the stone walls. In the same way the beautiful stone vaulting seen inside is another way of spanning spaces and transmitting the loads from these seeming diaphanous structures on to the surrounding walls, by means of ribs and arches in a pleasingly aesthetic way. For their day these structural forms were very innovative and daring, because of the ever-present danger of moving heavy materials into place without the disaster of collapse and loss of life.

There was however a lighter side to the story of the construction of the Cathedral. Bishop Walkelin was obliged to ask King William for timber, which existed in abundance in the forests around, with a view to mitigating some of the costs of the vast building programme. Permission was granted conditionally by the King to take from one of his woods, namely Hampage Wood, near Avington some five miles from Winchester, as much timber as could be felled and transported away in three days. The upshot of this arrangement was that all the trees within this wood were removed in the allotted time allowed apart from just one oak tree, the so-called "Gospel Oak", much to the chagrin of the King, or so the story goes!

Returning to the interior of the Cathedral and the **Crypt**; it is entered by a short flight of steps in the north transept and is situated beneath the Presbytery; its three aisles extend from the eastern side of the tower piers and again eastwards to the first piers of the Retro-choir. This

Above the Presbytery
These flying buttresses and soaring stone pinnacles above the Presbytery exemplify the structural genius of the medieval builders, by which masonry dead loads from high level, are transmitted safely to the foundations, without distortion of the main fabric, with a seemingly effortless grace.

extensive subterranean chamber extends eastwards with two further smaller crypts. The main crypt has circular stone piers supporting a simple vaulted roof in what, overall, has been described as "*rude Norman style*". The whole structure is raised up beneath the east end of the original Norman Cathedral with the high altar placed immediately above.

The crypt, because of its low elevation in relation to the ground water-table, is liable to flooding and in this respect actually contains a well. These factors, taken together, are a cogent indication of the difficult ground conditions on which the Cathedral foundations rest, a matter which came startlingly to light at the beginning of the century when serious faults appeared, principally at the east end of the Cathedral and within the crypt structure itself. (This was not the first time that the foundations had failed because in 1107 the central tower had actually collapsed and had to be rebuilt. At that time it was more convenient to attribute the disaster, *"to be a judgement for the sin of burying in this sacred precinct of* the *church the body of King William Rufus"* the much hated monarch.

On leaving the crypt the dramatic **North Transept** comes into view, being part of the original Norman Cathedral built on the traditional three levels of the arcade at ground level, with the triforium at the intermediate stage and surmounted by the clerestory, beneath the flat timber ceiling painted in the typical Norman tradition. The Rev. Telford Varley writing in 1909 aptly identifies the character of this architectural style. *"It is no light burden that these pillars hold aloft, nor do they support their burdens joyously or even with ease - each one an Atlas bearing his load strongly and uncomplainingly, but needing to put all his powers in the effort".* Having said this, however, there is a subtle sense of contrast in this area between the robustness of the stonework and the lightness of the ceiling. Located in this area are both the **Epiphany and Holy Sepulchre Chapels**, the former for private prayer for those who remember that this building is first and foremost the House of God, the latter being the repository of 12th century wall paintings showing the Deposition and Entombment of Christ.

Moving eastwards along the North Ambulatory, there are sideways views of the great Presbytery and the High Altar. Behind and set to the rear of the High Altar are **Bishop Gardiner's Chantry Chapel** facing the North Ambulatory, and on the other side **Bishop Fox's Chantry Chapel** looking towards the South Ambulatory. Bishop Stephen Gardiner was Bishop of Winchester from 1531-51 and 1553-55, and in this Cathedral officiated at the marriage of Prince Philip of Spain and Queen Mary Tudor, in 1554. Bishop Richard Fox was buried in his Chantry on the day of his death at Wolvesey on the 5th October 1528,

Vaulted ceilings in the Retrochoir
The simplicity of the vaulting in the 12th Century Retrochoir is in contrast with the flamboyant 15th Century remodelling of the vaulting in the Ladychapel.

The Crypt
A view of the Crypt shows evidence of the waterlogged ground conditions, on which the Cathedral foundations sit. The statue is modern and is by the sculptor Antony Gormley entitled "Sound 11".

with specific instructions whereby *"fifty torches are to accompany his body to the burying",* in other words a spectacular departure!

Beyond the High Altar, the interventions and additions of **Bishop De Lucy** (1189-1204) were planned in the Early English Gothic style forming the **Retrochoir**. towards the east end. At this stage, the change in style brings with it a welcome sense of lightness to the interior and with it also a change of scale to more human proportions. The overall space subdivides into nine bays, each one spanned by simple ribbed vaulting, which descends in turn on to beautiful piers composed of clusters of Purbeck Marble shafts, set around a central octagonal column elegantly banded at mid height. At floor level are some similarly beautiful floors of geometrical tiling, also dating from the 13th century, being the oldest and largest area of encaustic tiles to survive in England.

The building of the Retrochoir came about to accommodate pilgrims to **St. Swithun's Shrine,** who by all accounts came in great numbers in medieval times. They were allowed access to the Cathedral by a door in the North Transept called the Pilgrim's Door, which is now blocked up; although iron screens curtailed access beyond into the main body of the Cathedral. The mortal remains of St. Swithun were commemorated by a shrine located in the Retrochoir in 1476, although this was demolished in 1538, while today the spot is marked by a modest and modern memorial to Winchester's most famous saint.

Beyond the Retrochoir, the **Ladychapel** is flanked to the north by the **Guardian Angel's Chapel** and to the south by **Bishop Langton's Chapel.** The Ladychapel itself is quite notable for displaying some painted wall panels on the subject of the Golden Legend relating to the Blessed Virgin, dating from about 1500, and executed under the direction

The North Transept
Print of an original engraving circa 1836 by W. Griffith from a drawing by R. Garland showing the Norman work of Bishop Walkelin, (1070-98), before the addition of Epiphany Chapel. (Author's Collection)

of Prior Silkestede. There is an interesting panel in which the Blessed Virgin instructs the master builder of the Cathedral how to construct a capstan, in order to lift heavy building materials into position

The Guardian Angel's Chapel is an exquisite gem, resplendent with the heads of angels executed in very delicate colours of ochre, green and gold. The figureheads were painted by the artist Master William in about the year

The Retrochoir
Print of an original engraving circa 1836 by W. E. Albutt from a drawing by R. Garland. A perspective of the Retrochoir looking east, with the Chantry of Cardinal Henry Beaufort (1404-47), and Bishop William Waynflete (1447-86), to the south and north respectively. The Ladychapel is in the background. (Author's Collection).

1240 during the reign of King Henry III, with such artistry that the images leave a lasting impression. The same can be said of the whole ambience of the Retrochoir wherein lies the tomb of Bishop Godfrey de Lucy, (1189-1209), whose flair and imagination helped inspire this holy space.

Returning westwards along the South Ambulatory on the right, the view of the great Presbytery comes into focus again, leading towards this breathtakingly dramatic

inner sanctum. To the east is the **High Altar and Great Screen,** (c1455-75), while to the west is the enclosed space of the Choir, divided from the nave by George Gilbert Scott's Choir Screen. Above is the crossing beneath the great Norman Tower. It is not possible to over emphasize the power of the inter-relationship between the spaces here. This is the focus of the entire Cathedral, with all the intricate architectural detail providing a serene setting for the spiritual function of this great church, in which for some 900 years it has been a revered place of worship.

It has been suggested the crossing marks the division between the private section of the Cathedral by a screen, or "pulpitum", separating the choir (quire) and clergy to the east and the congregation in the west. The same theory continues to propose that the original monks' quarters to the east would have been more severe in character while the public areas of the nave would have been elaborately decorated with murals and painted symbols. In this way it would have provided a suitable setting for religious festivals in the Middle Ages, not unlike the banners which currently adorn the nave.

Perhaps one of the most interesting features in the Choir and Presbytery is the vaulting, which to all intents and purposes looks like stone, whereas it is in fact built in wood to appear like stone. The reason for this stems from the rebuilding of the tower following its collapse and the need to reduce the weight of the roof structure on the surrounding walls. This vaulting was the brainchild of **Bishop Richard Fox,** (1501-28), who was also responsible for adding the stone parclose screens and Presbytery aisles, reredos, and new east window. The vaulting is in a configuration called *"lierne"*, being a sophisticated system of simulated stone ribs with bosses to conceal the joints at the intersections, and with these bosses bolted on and being

23

The alterations to the arches of the nave

Drawing of the alterations to the Nave *carried out by William of Wykeham, from details prepared by Professor Willis for the Archaeological Institute at Winchester in 1845.*

View from the Triforium Gallery *looking down towards the Nave as altered by Bishop William of Wykeham in the late 14th Century.*

carved and painted quite brilliantly. The themes of these carvings encompass the crucifixion and elsewhere some seemingly macabre images, which may be out of place in a church, but it is thought that they are there to symbolise sin and the consequences thereof. In addition there are more conventional themes with coats of arms, including the Royal Coat of Arms and Garter, Arms of Fox as Bishop of Winchester as well as Arms of the See of Winchester. Beneath the tower vault of the Cathedral is an exquisitely carved and painted roof boss, which depicts King Charles 1 (reigned from 1625-49) and his Queen all executed in bright heraldic colours of red, white and blue; with gold for the inscription; reminding the visitor to look upwards in this building to appreciate the subtlety of the artistry of the heavenward view.

Within the Choir and Presbytery there are some notable items of craftsmanship again created from timber. Without doubt, the most spectacular of these are the **Choir Stalls** dating from about 1308, and reputedly carved by one William Lyngwode. There are romantic pastoral images, in other words non-religious subjects; although such motifs were quite common in the Middle Ages especially in the pews of parish churches where the joy of a good harvest is sometimes recorded for posterity. To the immediate east of the choir stalls is the **Choir Pulpit**, a

St. Swithun's Shrine
The original shrine was destroyed on the orders of Thomas Cromwell on the 21st September 1528, and in a letter from his Private Secretary Thomas Wriothesley it states, "At about 3 o'clock this Saturday morning we made an end to the shrine here at Winchester". In other words the deed was done under the cover of darkness!

flamboyant and over- elaborately carved piece, carrying the name of Prior Silkestede (1498-1524), with the **Bishop's Throne** on the west side of the stalls, early 19th century in origin, by William Garbett.

At the west end of the Cathedral and within the nave there is an architectural conundrum to be explained. Whereas the whole of the nave is in the glorious Perpendicular Gothic style of the 14th Century, it masks the original Norman nave of William Walkelin and was the subject of some monumental remodelling conceived by Bishop William Edington (1345-66), and executed to completion by Bishop William of Wykeham (1366-1404). During the period of the two bishoprics, the length of the nave was shortened and the twin west towers removed, and the original Norman work reshaped, in a way which would be unthinkable today, and yet what a splendid "tour de force" has been handed down to our generation.

William of Wykeham employed the renowned mason **William Wynford** to oversee and direct this remarkable project. The original configuration of the nave was transformed from the three-tier system of arcade at floor level, triforium at intermediate stage and clerestorey at the summit into a two-tier arrangement. Soaring perpendicular arches surmounted by webs of stone tracery concealed the blank walls behind (of Norman origin) with new perpendicular windows above. The entire arrangement was climaxed by the lierne stone vaulting linking the north and south ranges of the nave with the aisles beyond. The overall height to the apex of the nave vaulting equals some 23.5 metres and the total width of both nave and the two aisles is of the order of 26.8 metres.

Within the nave itself is the **Chantry Chapel of William of Wykeham,** both built and dedicated in his lifetime, and situated in the central bay of the south aisle, where it is recorded that he was buried in 1404 on the 27th

Chantry Chapel of Bishop William of Wykeham (1366-1404)
This serene image of a powerful churchman protected in death by iron railings, within a tomb and chapel of supreme opulence.

West Window

*This is by far the largest
window in the Cathedral, and
is made up of fragments of
stained glass collected after the
windows were broken by
Oliver Cromwell's troops.
However, the architectural
composition of the tracery
remains unaltered in the 3:3:3
rhythm of its mullions and is
thereafter subdivided into 44
fields and arranged on 6 levels.
Internally, this fine window is
seen in close juxtaposition with
the lierne vaulting of the nave
roof and the two-tier
arrangement of the nave
arcades.*

The Norman Font
This 12ᵗʰ Century font of black Tournai Marble is one of four similar fonts in Hampshire. Historically, it is important for it shows an early illustration of a rudder attached to a ship's stern, and is a particularly appropriate image, in that the narrative frieze depicts scenes from the life of St. Nicholas, the patron saint of seamen and children.

Norman Font, Winchester Cathedral

of September. As part of his epitaph an inscription reads, *"Here, overthrown by death, lies William surnamed Wykeham. He was Bishop of this Church, and repairer of it"*. This statement is quite clearly an understatement in view of the massive changes he had brought about, partly to address the needs of maintenance of the structure but more in the zeal to build in a quintessentially English style.

The **Great West Window**, now denuded of much of its original stained glass figurative motives, following damage sustained in the Civil War period, is nevertheless an impressive architectural image of carved stone of some 44 major fields arranged on six levels culminating at the apex of the Perpendicular arch. Originally the stained glass depicted scenes from the life of Christ starting with the foretelling of his birth at the very top of the window, together with images of his Apostles through to his death and resurrection, although the precise format is now uncertain.

Within the south nave aisle is an interesting mason's

survey of the stone, (at the time of writing this book), in which it is recorded that the nave roof is comprised of Beer Stone, called "fields", between the ribs of the lierne vaults. There are bosses at the intersection of the ribs of these vaults which were secured in the 19th century by iron bolts, which having rusted have now been removed and replaced by stainless- steel connections. Much damage in medieval churches and cathedrals has resulted from the use of iron fixings in the stonework, mainly in Victorian times, causing subsequent failure when the material used to secure the stone has rusted and expanded. Interestingly it is recorded that no fewer than six different stones are identified in the aisle vaulting namely Portland, Caen, Beer, Bath, Doulting, and Quarr, the last mentioned being the stone source for the Norman Cathedral. This, therefore, provides evidence of the ongoing repair programme over the centuries until the present day, hence the seemingly peripatetic sources of the stones used.

One of the finest of the stone treasures within the

The Morley Library
This room, situated at high level in the South Transept of the Cathedral, contains over 2000 books presented by Bishop George Morley, (1662-84), and each of his books is identified by the monogram "M".

The wood for the shelving is oak from the Alice Holt Forest and was installed originally at the Bishop's Palace at Farnham.

Cathedral must be the sombre **Norman Font,** (one of four in Hampshire), dating from the 12th century, and made of black Tournai marble from Belgium. This font, thought to be the gift of Bishop Henry de Blois, is rectangular in plan, supported by a circular central drum, around which are four masonry shafts resting on a carved base. The beautiful carving around the four square sides of the font depicts the life of St. Nicholas, the patron saint of seamen, children and pawnbrokers. The font is sited between the nave columns of the north aisle, and is an ever-present reminder of the Christian tradition of baptism and formal entry into the world-wide family of Christ.

Finally, in the South Transept, where the Norman origins of this great Cathedral again confront the visitor, is found the entrance to the **Cathedral Library** and the **Triforium Gallery**. It is here that the priceless manuscripts and artistic artefacts are stored for safekeeping, including the Winchester School of Anglo-Saxon inspired illuminated manuscripts. In the Library are some two-thousand books and manuscripts presented by **Bishop George Morley** (1662-84). A treasured centrepiece of the collection is a copy of the 12th Century "**Winchester Bible**". At a higher level in the Triforium Gallery is a museum of Cathedral artefacts, including some late 15th century statuary from the Great Screen in the Presbytery,

The Triforium Gallery
This sculpture originally from the Great Altar Screen, depicts the Madonna and Child which was sculpted between 1479-1490, and is notable for, "It's realism and its extraordinary combination of divinity and humanity".

The Triforium Gallery
This is a further example of consummate stone carving by medieval masons, and depicts "Two dragons each biting the tail of the other", all part of an original roof boss.

showing signs of the aftermath of the actions of Cromwell's soldiers in the Civil War.

It is not possible in so short a space to describe in detail all that can be seen in this Cathedral, (which in any case has been minutely covered by previous writers), but it has been the intention here to think about the historic background to the creation of this undoubted ecclesiastical masterpiece; while pondering both on the financing and logistics of the building enterprise overall. Added to all this one must consider also the political forces brought about by changes in the monarchy as well as the personal idiosyncrasies of the Bishops concerned. This building is therefore an historical panorama in stone while at the same time being a record of great events and a place of worship. In conclusion, one story comes to mind of an incident at the time of the Battle of Waterloo, when by all accounts the news came first to Winchester by semaphore signals from the Cathedral tower. It was a misty day at the time and at first the message seen read, *"Wellington defeated"* but then the mist lifted and the remaining words emerged *"the enemy"*!

Within the south-east corner of the line of the Roman walls of the City, lie the remains of the great Palace of Wolvesey, where once stood the most important of the royal and ecclesiastical buildings of the Middle Ages. It was here there resided also some of the richest and most powerful bishops in the land, powerful not only in their pastoral role but also in the positions of high office in government. Although the origins of a palace on this site lay in Saxon times, the extensive remains seen today originate from the Norman era, when in accordance with the practice of the day, existing buildings were swept away. A new palace then arose to the designs of the second Norman bishop, **William Giffard** (1100-29). Bishop William had previously been Chancellor to King William Rufus (reigned 1087-1100) for the period 1093 until the King's untimely demise. His appointment to that of Bishop of Winchester followed the usual practice of that period in history, when service in high government office was rewarded by elevation to similarly high office within the Church establishment.

The boundaries of **Wolvesey Palace**, or Wolvesey Castle as it is sometimes known, (although it can more accurately be described as a fortified palace), are defined

Wolvesey Palace
These picturesque ruins, managed by English Heritage, are of the East Hall built by Bishop Henry de Blois in 1135-8 who created on this beautiful site " a house like a palace with a strong tower".

to the south and east by the line of the Roman city walls and to the west by one of the ancient watercourses, to which reference will be made later. To the north lay the site of **St. Mary's Abbey,** founded in A.D. 903, by Queen Aelhswith, King Alfred the Great's wife. Today the site, which is presented as a stabilised ruin, is managed by English Heritage, and is seen against a spectacular grassed area to the east now used as sports fields for the Pilgrim's School. Immediately to the west is the Palace of the present Bishop of Winchester within what is called the **"Baroque Palace"** which was restored to its present form and usage in 1928.

The buildings of Wolvesey fall primarily into four main bishopric eras. Namely that of Bishop William Giffard (1100-29), who initially built the West Hall, followed by Bishop Henry de Blois (1129-71) who was responsible for the major building of the great East Hall. Bishop William of Wykeham (1366-1404) then repaired and remodelled the Palace, and finally Bishop George Morley (1662-84) demolished the medieval Palace and built the south and west wings of the Baroque Palace. This Palace completed by Bishop Sir Jonathan Trelawney in (1707-21), part of which stands intact today, serves as the official residence of the present Bishop of Winchester.

Of the bishops reviewed above, the most outstanding contribution was made by **Henry de Blois**, upon whose background it would be well to ponder awhile since he was undoubtedly a man of exceptional ability and influence. He was born in circa the year 1090, the fourth son of Count Stephen of Blois and Chartres and his wife Adela (youngest daughter of William the Conqueror). At an early age he was sent to be educated at the Monastery in Cluny, and to train there as monk. Cluny had then a reputation for training men for high office and it was here that he became influenced by the doctrine concerning the need to maintain harmony between the State and Church. It was during his stay at Cluny that Henry gained a reputation for legal skills as well as being able to express his views lucidly in debate. At the same time he was surrounded by building works to Cluny Monastery being carried out in the Romanesque style of architecture, which influences can now be seen in the buildings of St. Cross, just outside Winchester, and elsewhere.

Henry de Blois, therefore, was a man of education with a religious training and an impeccable pedigree who was bound to succeed. It comes as no surprise that in 1126 he was appointed Abbot of Glastonbury and shortly afterwards in 1129 Bishop of the See of Winchester. With these dual appointments came great power and wealth

The "Baroque Palace"

View of the medieval chapel to the so-called "Baroque Palace" built by Bishop Morley who died in 1684. Today all that remains of this palace is the west wing built in the "Wren Style" and its 15th century Chapel, (standing on Norman foundations), with this perpendicular east facing window. Today this building is the home of the Bishop of Winchester

making him the richest Bishop, if not the wealthiest man, in the country. It was at Wolvesey that he made plans to build the great East Hall during the period 1135-8 when in the Winchester Annals it states "*in this year Bishop Henry created a house like a palace with a strong tower.*"

Today the remains of the medieval Palace are approached from a gateway in College Street along a pathway with the present Bishop's Palace on the left, and leading through an archway of trees to the place where the original entrance, outside the city walls, was located. Once inside the southern courtyard, the vista looking towards the remains of the great **East Hall built** by Henry de Blois is revealed. This is without doubt a splendid ruin and gives the visitor an impression of a past with significant grandeur. Bernard Woodward writing in 1860 says of these buildings, "*Perhaps the most interesting archaeological feature of these ruins of Wolvesey Castle is a peculiarity in the masonry of part of the walls.....*" and goes on to explain "*that a considerable part of the materials was obtained by the destruction of the palace built by William the Conqueror within the City, at the north western corner of the present cathedral cemetery,*" Be that as it may, other materials used included some Caen Stone from Normandy with the remainder from the quarry at Quarr in the Isle of Wight, while the bulk of the walls were built with local flint bonded with chalk. Because of the ponderous nature of the walls over a metre in thickness, taken together with the soggy nature of the ground, similar to that of the Cathedral nearby, it is said that the foundations were likewise built above a supporting structure of beech logs.

The layout of the Palace throughout its stages of evolution was collegiate in plan, i.e, arranged around a substantial courtyard. Here was a complex of buildings to administer the large manors and estates for which the Bishop was responsible, and to retain the records of these properties in what were called the "Pipe Rolls". In addition there were ancillary buildings such as barns, stables and a large wool-house. Because of the need to cater for large gatherings of people on ceremonial occasions, as well as the usual household, provision was made for a culverted water supply fed from wells within the complex. Additional infrastructure to the north- east is visible where there is an extensive latrine block discharging into what was known as Lock's Pond.

Some great ceremonial events were enacted within these walls, and in the area occupied by de Blois's kitchen a plaque records a royal feast held on 5th February 1403 to celebrate the meeting of Henry 1V (reigned 1399-1413) and Joan of Navarre. The menu included such delicacies as "*cygnets, capons, venison with furmente, rabbits, pullets, partridges, woodcock, plover, quail, snipe, fieldfares, roast kid, custards, fritters, cream of almonds, pears in syrup, and subtleties with crowns and eagles*" in all costing £552-12s-0p. Bearing in mind that in medieval times a pound sterling amounted to a pound weight in solid silver, 240 pennies were equivalent to one pound and the average wage of, for example, a farm labourer amounted at that time to a few pence per day, the enormity of such extravagance in modern day terms can be measured.

The works carried out by **Bishop William of Wykeham** (1366-1404) were at a time when the Palace had fallen into a poor state of repair. Holding and repair works were carried out during the years 1372-3 including improvements to the moat, a new curtain wall was constructed on the east side adjacent to Wymond's Tower and the Keep, and facilities upgraded in the East Hall kitchen by the addition of a "salsary" where sauces were to be prepared. At the same time there was to be a complete remodelling of the Bishop's apartments in the southern part of the West Hall. All in all, it can be said that this era marked the total refurbishment of the Palace. Afterwards a decline was to follow brought about by the failure of succeeding bishops to properly maintain the extensive fabrics from the end of the 15th Century and thereafter.

The final chapter in this saga comes with the advent of **Bishop George Morley's** decision to build a new Palace in the Baroque style in the 1680's to be known as the

"Baroque Palace". A design is illustrated by a drawing by one William Cove as published in "**The History and Antiquities of Winchester**" which work was to be completed by Morley's successor **Bishop Jonathan Trelawney** in 1715. Again, however, the ravages of time took their toll and this Palace was demolished in part, leaving only the west wing, which was later restored and altered in 1928.

Today Wolvesey (the present Bishop's residence) stands resplendent behind two stone piers and wrought iron entrance gates giving views of the grandeur of the Palace that once was. (Now specifically dated by Pevsner/ Lloyd as 1684). The Bishop's Palace is two storeys in height, of ashlar stonework pierced by what are described as wooden-cross windows, while above is an imposing clay tile roof surmounted by discreet dormers and soaring chimney stacks. Beyond this there is the Chapel at right angles standing on its Norman foundations, with its Perpendicular Gothic windows, set at first- floor level in the piano nobile position, as is the norm for palace chapels. This building overlooks the ruins of the old palaces, and standing in this venerable place, the atmosphere of all that has gone before pervades the very air. As the Cathedral bells ring out to break the silence of the magic of this place, one is again reminded of the words *"Bishop Henry created a house like a palace"*, a fitting epitaph for a man of vision and immaculate taste.

The Bishop's Palace
A view from the surviving west wing of Wolvesey, which since 1928 has been used as the home of the Bishops of Winchester.

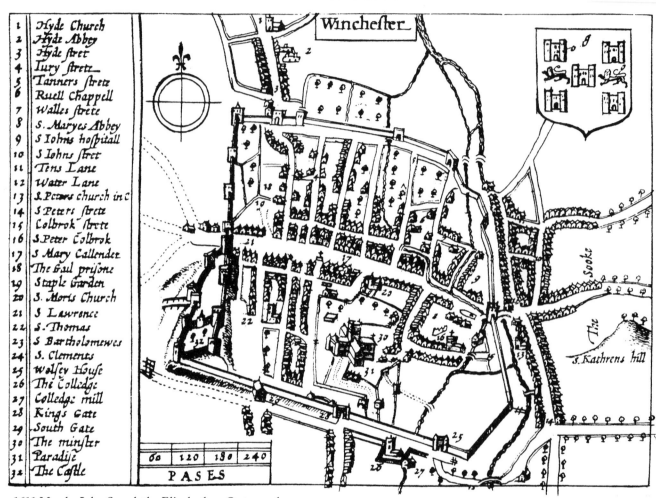

1	Hyde Church
2	Hyde Abbey
3	Hyde stret
4	Iury strete
5	Tanners strete
6	Ruell Chappell
7	Walles strete
8	S. Maryes Abbey
9	S Iohns hospitall
10	S Iohns stret
11	Tens Lane
12	Water Lane
13	S. Peters church in C
14	S Peters strete
15	Colbrok strete
16	S.Peter Colbrok
17	S Mary Callender
18	The Gail prisone
19	Staple Garden
20	S. Moris Church
21	S Lawrence
22	S. Thomas
23	S Bartholomewes
24	S. Clements
25	Wolsey House
26	The Colledge
27	Colledge mill
28	Kings Gate
29	South Gate
30	The minster
31	Paradise
32	The Castle

1611 Map by John Speed, the Elizabethan Cartographer
Reproduced by Courtesy of J. M. Dent and Son Ltd.
From The Story of Winchester", by W. Lloyd Woodland. First
Edition 1932. (Author's Collection).

Chapter 3

WINCHESTER'S STREET PATTERNS
AND NOTABLE BUILDINGS

The first reliable map of Winchester can be seen in the early 17th century map by **John Speed**, the Elizabethan cartographer. The Roman and Saxon origins of the layout of the streets of the city have already been touched upon in the first chapter of this book. The planning of the shape of the town by the diversion of the River Itchen and the inclusion of part of Oram's Arbour, and the later Saxon grid plan layout of the streets, within a Roman fortified enclosing wall, is in essence the shape seen today. This fortified and compact configuration of the city plan is recorded in this map by Speed, showing the town wall and protecting ditch, and the line of the present-day High Street and Broadway travelling west to east. Radiating from this spine road are the arms of the grid-iron pattern, pointing both north and south. Within this overall configuration are the familiar features of the Cathedral to the east, and the remains of the castle fortifications to the west. In addition, the sites of the medieval churches and street patterns carried through to the present day, are clearly seen. Outside the confines of the walls and watch-towers are the sites of Hyde Abbey to the north and Winchester College to the south. The locations of the town's gates to the north, south, west and the east demonstrate the secure points of access to the town, and its overall location in its relationship with the River Itchen.

Speed's map is an early example of map-making of a more advanced state, with its scale marked in "pases" (paces). The University of Southampton holds an illuminated Elizabethan map of Southampton, which however, is totally inaccurate when it comes to scale. Like the Southampton map, Speed's version of Winchester does seek to represent both landscape and buildings three-dimensionally, as seen from above. It was not until the very beginning of the 19th century, when the Ordnance Survey moved from its fire-damaged base at the Tower of London to Southampton, that scientific and accurate map-making became universally available and the norm.

In an "**Ancient Ichnography of the City of Winchester**", published on March 1st 1809, there is a representation of what in effect is the medieval layout of the city. The lines of the roads, ditch and encircling walls, Castle ramparts, Cathedral precincts, with the College to the south and Hyde Abbey to the north, are all clearly shown. This plan reflects the information given in Speed's map, 200 years earlier, but in much more detail. Of further interest, residential developments outside the confines of the city walls appear at this date. Beyond the East Gate and across the River Itchen there is a substantial concentration of buildings leading to St. Giles' Hill and in the roads running parallel with the river. This, however, was indicated also in Speed's map but not in such detail. The open spaces of the water meadows around Winchester College also remain as a backdrop to Wykeham's buildings, before their expansion in later years.

Moving forward but a short distance in time to

THIS City stands pleasantly on y̆ beautiful banks of y̆ river Itchin, y̆ contains about a mile y̆ a half within y̆ Walls, besides y̆ Suburbs; 'twas y̆ famous city of y̆ t̆
Roman Emperors seem to have had at this place, their Imperial weaving shops, where y̆ Cloaths for y̆ Emperors; y̆ y̆ Army, as well as Sails for their Ships, Linnen y̆ other neceȷ̆
his father Constantine, y̆ who usurp'd y̆ Government in opposition to Honorious. In y̆ Heptarchy 'twas y̆ seat of y̆ West Saxon Kings, y̆ their burial place. K. Cenemalch (aft̆
made Bishop A.D.1073 erected a Cathedral after y̆ same model, (tho much more stately as Malmesbury observes) y̆ arch'd it with stone. His Succeȷ̆ors, contributed to its beauty y̆
Bishop Fox did y̆ East end from y̆ Tower to y̆ High altar. 'twas commended to y̆ Patronage of several, viz, Amphibalus, S.t Peter, S.t Swithin y̆ lastly of y̆ Holy Trinity; There wer̆
to S.t Edburg An. Val. £179:7:2 Edn.d y̆ elder pursuiant to his father K. Alfreds will founded a College of secular Canons here which was call'd y̆ New Minster, but they were
1301 a College for a Provost, 6 Priests, y̆ 6 Clerks which was dedicated to S.t Eliz. An. Val. £112:17:4 ob: William of Wickham, beforemention'd establish'd A.D.1387 a College t̆
16 Choiristers y̆ y̆ Statutable Servants. Hen. Beaufort Bishop here, half brother to Hen. IV founded an Alms house within y̆ precincts of S.t Croȷ̆es: but he dying before it was establiȷ̆
Poverty; establish'd near Winchester by Hen. Cardinal of England y̆ Bishop of Winchester, son of John late Duke of Lancaster. An. Val. £84:4:4. This City sends two Burgeȷ̆es t̆

Engraving by S. and N. Buck, 1736 entitled "The East Prospect of the City of Winchester".

This print of the engraving is by far the most tangible three dimensional image of Winchester at the beginning of the 18th Century, the details of which are confirmed by the later map of 1809 by J. Cave and J. Milner. It was not until the 1840's that William Henry Fox Talbot first produced photographs to record such images accurately for posterity. (Reproduced by courtesy of the Hampshire Record Office.)

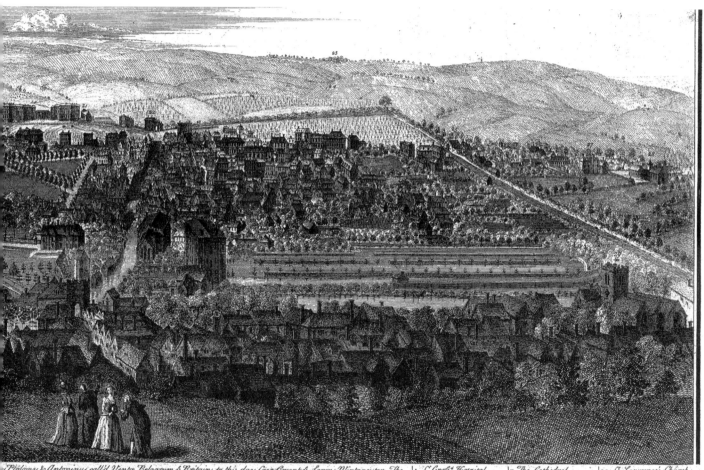

Ptolomy & Antoninus call'd Venta Belgarum, & Britains to this day Caer-Grvent, & Saxons Wintancister. The or their houses were wove Here liv'd that Constans & Monk, who was first made Cæsar, & afterwards Emperor by & Roman age was destroy'd / built here A.D. 643 a Church very splendid for those times, on & Site whereof Walkelin articulary William de Edington & William de Wickham, who built & West part of & Church from & Choir, as days, other religious Houses here viz a Benedictine Nunnery built A.D. 900 by Alswitha consort to K. Alfred, dedicated Adam Martin erected a Monastery to & honour of St James. John de Pontysar Bishop of this See, founded A.D. V. Mary consisting of a Warden, 10 Fellows 1 Schoolmaster 1 Usher & 70 Scholars, 3 Chaplains 3 Clerks 1 Organist incorporated the Members therein under a Rector of their own By the name of the New Alms House of Noble are Paulet St John & George Bridges Esqrs. ——— Saml & Nathl Buck delin. et Sculp. according to Act of Parliament 1736.

1. St Cross Hospital	11. The Cathedral	20. St Lawrence's Church
2. Navigable River from Southamp	12. Bowling Green	21. The County Hall
3. Black Bridge	13. St James's burying Ground	22. West Gate
4. Rumsey Road	14. The Kings Palace	23. Lainston
5. The College	15. St Thomas's Church	24. Stockbridge Road
6. The Bishop's Palace	16. East Gate	25. The North Gate
7. Remains of Wolsey Palace	17. St Johns House	26. Bowling Green
8. St Michael's Church	18. The Hospital for	27. Hide House
9. St Peter's Church in & Soke	Clergymen's Widows	28. St Bartholomew's Church
10. South Gate	19. St Maurice's Church	29. St John's Church in & Soke

1850-60, the map of this date, now held by the Hampshire Record Office, still reflects the medieval plan of the city with the High Street as its focus and spine road, harking back also to its Roman origins. The Saxon road pattern was superimposed on the previous Roman "grid-iron" plan which was centred on the "Forum", which lay just to the south of the present-day High Street. The Saxon streets were laid out circa A.D. 880 with branch roads radiating outwards and at right angles to the High Street, both to the north and to the south. The purpose of this ordered layout was primarily defensive, providing a clear view at any one central place to the perimeter of the city, in times of conflict or onslaught from outside. The main addition to the city plan appears at this time in the guise of the railway, (the South-Western Railway), gently passing the main conurbation to the west. The main **Railway Station,** designed by Sir William Tite, is shown sited to the north-west, but giving reasonable ease of access to the centre, with an additional platform serving the Peninsula Barracks. Of special interest, to the west of the railway, the site of the remainder of Oram's Arbour is shown surviving the original Roman plans to reshape the city. The main significance of the emergence of the railway is the dramatic effect on communication and the movement of people and goods in the wake of the Industrial Revolution in this country

The **High Street,** its name derived from Roman times to denote a paved carriage-way set above the general level of the terrain, forms the backbone of the Winchester system. It is not entirely straight in form, with gentle and subtle curves in its progress from the Westgate, downwards through to The **Broadway** and its end at the City Bridge over the River Itchen. From the river up-wards towards the city centre there is a gradual gradient, and after the wide spaces of the Broadway at the east, there is also a general narrowing and tightness between the buildings on either side. Because of the orientation the facades on the south side face northwards, and are in a shade punctuated only by the openings created by the intersecting side roads. This light and shade creates much visual interest, especially when combined with the unexpected opening up of spaces along the way, for instance at the Buttercross. At this point an additional view opens up southwards, through the passageway leading to Cathedral Green, together with glimpses of Great Minster Street. It was on this same spot that **William the Conqueror's Palace** once stood, a fact recorded on a wall facing the west door of St. Lawrence Church.

At the Westgate, where the High Street ends, there is a comprehensive view of the city looking eastwards, where its historic main thoroughfare is framed against the lush green backdrop of St. Giles' Hill. Alongside this view, the side streets spread out like straight fingers, with such historic names harking back to either the trades carried on there, or more often the physical character of each place. In addition as circumstances and usages have changed so have the street names. For instance **Jewry Street,** initially famous for the Jewish community in the city in the 13th century, was renamed Jail Street in the 17th century with the building of a prison there, and subsequently reverted to its original name when the prison was re-sited in the Romsey Road. **St Peter's Street** was first called "Fleshmongers", **Southgate Street** originally named "Gold Street", and **St. Thomas Street** "Calpe" based on the Anglo-Saxon word for silver. Perhaps the most aptly named streets in Winchester are **Lower, Middle and Upper Brook Streets,** where once streams ran down the middle of each road, as seen in the "Buck" engraving of 1736.

Although the streets of modern Winchester are paved,

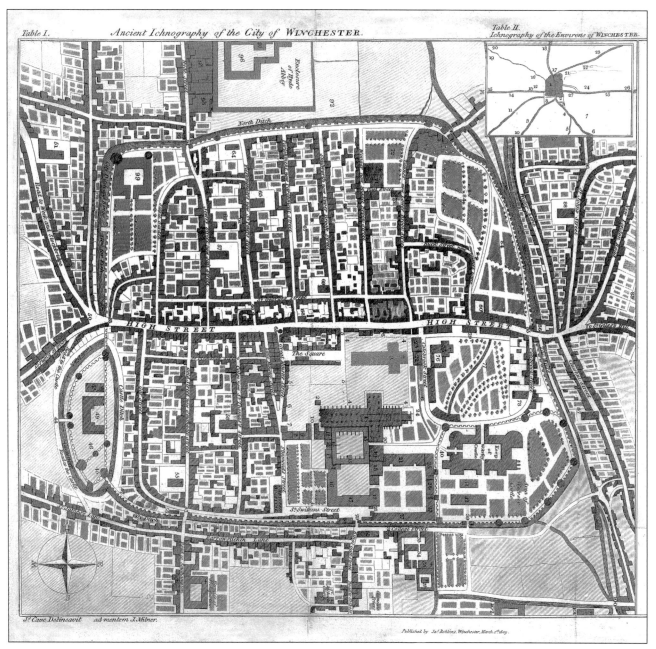

Ancient Ichnography of the City of Winchester 1809,
by J. Cave and J. Milner.
(Author's Collection).

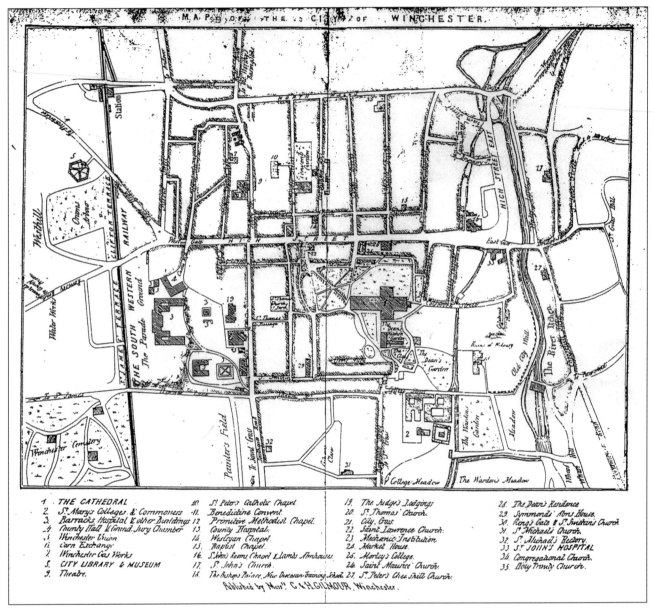

Map of the City of Winchester 1850-60

(Reproduced by Courtesy of the Hampshire Record Office.)

cleaned, drained and with street lighting to illuminate the night, this was not always the case. In medieval times these refinements hardly existed, if at all. Owners of individual properties were expected to make their own arrangements, and the accumulation of rubbish upon the roads was a particular problem, as was the lack of any made-up surfaces. It was not until the setting up of the Paving Commission in 1770, that in the first instance the High Street was paved with "a good surface of flints", and similarly footpaths provided for pedestrians. In addition, provision was then made for some street lighting, numbering of houses (originally identified by the owner's name), and efforts made with only partial success to drain the sloping High Street. In other words, civilising influences stirred for the first time to bring order where disorder once held sway. However, today, modern traffic is the enemy of the environment, especially in an historic setting, and in this respect Winchester is no exception, notwithstanding pedestrianisation and traffic management schemes in place.

Turning now to the buildings in the streets of Winchester. Much has been written and recorded, but here it is intended to give an overview of the most significant of these historic edifices. In The Broadway, to the east of the High Street, the **Guildhall** in its imposing Victorian splendour cannot be overlooked. Designed by the architects

The Guildhall
Designed by the Architects
Jeffery and Skiller in 1871-3
and extended in 1892-3.
(To the far right is the original
School of Art designed by
Thomas Stopher in 1875.)

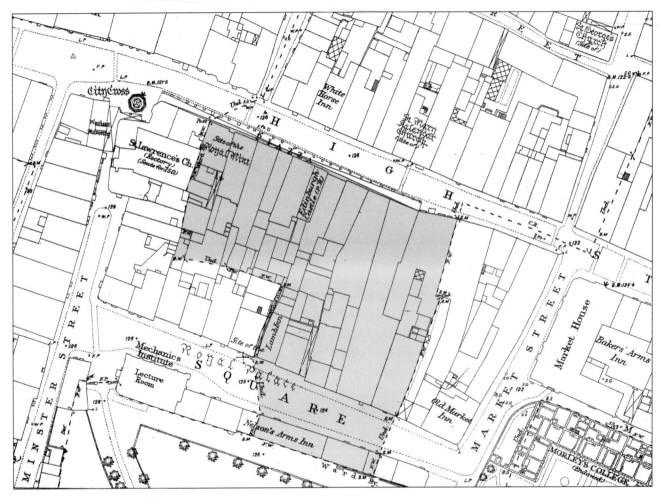

Ordnance Survey Map, 1873

This extract from the Ordnance Survey Map of 1873 shows the
sites of Market House, the Pentice, (Piazza), and the Buttercross,
(City Cross). In addition, the sites of the former Royal Mint and
Royal Palace of William the Conqueror are indicated.
The historical importance of these maps cannot be over emphasised
being an accurate encapsulation of Victorian Winchester.
(Reproduced by courtesy of the Hampshire Local Studies
Collection, County Library and the Ordnance Survey.)

Jeffery and Skiller in 1871-3, it was extended in 1892-3 to further designs by J.B. Colson. It is a truly remarkable "tour de force", in a seemingly French Gothic style, with walls of pink and cream sandstone and surmounted by a steeply sloping patterned slate roof, with a soaring central clock tower and precipitously sloping roof above. The principal rooms are at first-floor level and approached by both outer and inner staircases, the latter beneath a triple arched portico. It is recorded that the cost of the main building was £10,313.00, and the rear extension was built for just £4,837.00. A plaque in the main entrance records that the Rt. Hon. Lord Selborne, Lord High Chancellor of Great Britain, opened the Guildhall on the 14th of May 1873. Nearby, on the wall of the staircase outside, the foundation stone was laid by the Rt. Hon. Lord Viscount Eversley on the 22nd of December 1871. In other words the entire building was completed in just a year and a half, a truly remarkable achievement for the city.

Perhaps one of the most interesting features internally is in the details of the deep vaulted lobby behind the arched portico. The Gothic stone arches, ribs and capitals with red and yellow-banded brick "fields" or panels of the vaults, demonstrate the Victorian's love of pomp and ceremony and in its detail their preoccupation with bright colours.

Market House in the High Street is situated at the junction with Market Street where it turns the corner looking towards the Cathedral. It was built in 1857 in the Greek Doric Revival style and was designed by the then City Engineer, William Coles. This is a small but visually powerful building, and although diminished by modern additions, it nevertheless represents a potent image in the street scene with its robust stone façade and detailing. In landscape terms it leads the eye to the Pentice further to

Market House
Built in 1857 in the Greek Doric style. A corner detail, where stonework for the main façade changes to a mellow red brick on the Market Street elevation. This building was formerly home to the "Green Market" where traders sold fruit and vegetables.

the west on the same side of the street.

The row of shops forming the **Pentice**, or Piazza as it was once called, is notable for its covered walkway, with shop-fronts set back from the main line of the building above, and a row of supporting circular columns against the street. In appearance this arrangement has a similarity in its architectural form with the medieval "Rows" in Chester, but without its two-storey arrangement. This configuration gives protection from inclement weather, but being north-facing the walkway is in a state of perpetual semi shade. However, the walkway remains attractive because of its unique and cosy image and forms part of the visual and architectural variety for which this street is justly famous.

Immediately beyond the Pentice, and set back in a small recess, the **Buttercross** comes into view. Built in the 15th Century, this cross marks the focus of trade in medieval Winchester, and in simplistic terms the name is said to originate from the sale of butter at this spot, or another explanation is that it was the only place where butter could be consumed in Lent. Be that as it may, it is certainly an elaborate and imposing stone structure with central human figures inside and at the very summit a cross, giving credence to the idea of some religious significance hand-in-hand with trade. It was in this part of the High Street that specialist shops were located in medieval times. These trades included fishmongers, saddlers, butchers, parmenters (skinners), goldsmiths and drapers as well as "dubbers" or dyers. This was the location of the 12th Century mint where the "moneyers" plied their trade. Winchester at that time was a centre for the money market in this country, started by the Jewish community in Jewry Street, until their expulsion in 1290. Winchester merchants used these financial services to fund credit to their

The Pentice
The colonnade of slender columns support the mainly 16th century timber framed buildings, (some re-fronted), while the covered way gives welcome protection from the weather, all contributing to "its unique and cosy image".

The Old Guildhall, now Lloyds TSB

A view of the rooftop cupola and unusual illuminated clock, cantilevered over the pavement. Below and to the left of the clock is a statue of Queen Anne, (Reigned 1702-14), set between a range of elegant sash windows, with solid Tuscan stone columns below, framing the arched windows.

customers, very much like the system existing today. In addition both the Church and the State borrowed money from these same sources. The currency was based on the "Pound Sterling", related to a pound weight in silver, with the shilling 1/20th in value and the penny 12 parts of a shilling. The money market is reflected in the name of a nearby street namely Calpe (silver) Street, where these moneyers lived (now called St. Thomas Street).

Leaving the Buttercross and moving past buildings around the west side of St. Lawrence Church and into Great Minster Street, **The Square** adjacent to the Cathedral, comes into view.

It is here that the medieval markets flourished in the north west corner of the churchyard. It was also the place for gatherings and merry-makings on appropriate occasions although also infamous for smells from the Royal Mint, (smelting), and rubbish left over from the markets! Justice was also administered here in the form of the town pillory and stocks sited adjacent to the present City Museum. In Norman times, William the Conqueror's Palace stood here also, although lost to posterity when its stones were used to build Wolvesey Palace on the orders of Bishop Henry de Blois. An outline of this Palace can be seen on the Victorian Ordnance Map of 1871. Today there is a tight enclave of streets in a small rectangle formed by the top end of Great Minster Street, The Square and Market Street leading back into the High Street passing Market House.

The history of commerce and trade within the City of Winchester is reflected in the guilds, which regulated the trades carried on here. These guilds were modelled, it is thought, on similar organisations in London, with whom traders would have engaged in business. Locally the civic authorities had an ulterior motive for supporting such

The Buttercross
This elegant 15th century carved stone structure, some 14 metres high, was restored in 1865 by the architect George Gilbert Scott, and contains, amongst others, statues of William of Wykeham and King Alfred.

guilds in order to protect their own financial interest, i.e. revenue from trade. However the guilds were essentially there in medieval times to control prices and the quality of goods sold, and to maintain the good name of the city. It was here that regulation of Sunday trading first appeared, on which day tradesmen were not allowed to carry on their business with the exception of shops selling perishable food and then only during certain hours. Trade therefore, at this time was properly regulated and organised, and being a member of a recognised guild was indeed an honour.

At the junction of Great Minster Street and The Square is the **Winchester City Museum**, built in 1902, and occupying the site of the old Mechanics Institute and Lecture Room. Among its very fine exhibits are displays relating to the trade of the city. For instance, there is a scenic restoration of Hunt's the Chemist, situated in the High Street until 1980. The original mahogany counters and "lancet" doors are seen, together with a range of apparatus for the dispensing of medicines. Included in the display are the traditional glass "carboys" filled with coloured water to advertise the shop. Again there is a similar display of the tobacco merchant Foster and Son, sited in the Pentice since 1871, and further moved in 1980, a bad year for conservation or so it would seem! The Roman display on the top floor of the museum is quite breathtaking with the fine mosaic floor taken from the excavations at the "Brooks" shopping centre development. The museum in which so much of Winchester's history is both recorded and saved, is designed in a contemporary version of the Tudor style. Externally there are flint walls and mellow stone dressings to the transoms and mullions of the windows and at the main door; reminiscent of the style adopted for the Castle Hill Offices built a little earlier. (The whole building has received a complete makeover and re-arrangement of exhibits, since the writing of this book.)

Returning to the High Street via the Buttercross, and moving westwards along the present-day pedestrian precinct, there are two notable buildings namely the **Old Guildhall** (now Lloyds TSB), and the other the **offices of the Hampshire Chronicle**. The Old Guildhall was traditionally, since circa 1361, the place where the "Hall of Court" cases were heard in the Court of Record before the

Offices of the Hampshire Chronicle at 57 High Street
This building, with its bow windows at ground floor level, makes a unique contribution to the street scene.

Mayor and two bailiffs. The present building dates from 1712-13. Its classical façade of red brick and stone embellishments is surmounted by a statue of Queen Anne (reigned 1702-14), and above this is a large cantilevered illuminated clock. At the highest level is a cupola lined with lead and above this a weathervane. Over the years the uses of this building have changed and in 1835 it served as meeting place for the Corporation until the present Guildhall was opened in 1873. A plaque on the side of the present building reads *"Here hangs the City Curfew Clock, which is still rung at 8 p.m. each weekday"*.

The Hampshire Chronicle building houses the

Winchester Offices of the newspaper founded in 1771. It has a traditional cream rendered façade punctuated by black painted windows all nestling comfortably beneath a plain tiled roof. At ground floor level and facing the pavement there are bow windows, and overall this building makes a unique contribution to the character of the High Street in that it has not suffered from the addition of a modern shopfront. At the top end of the High Street, in close proximity to the Westgate, are the **Offices of the Hampshire County Architect,** the centrepiece of which is number 77, where the stucco façade is painted in two tones of light cream and yellow. This is a classical building with pilasters through two storeys, above deep rustications at ground floor level. However because of its north-facing ambience, the colours look cheerful on the dullest of days, and avoid the tradition of painting stucco to replicate stone.

At the intersection of Jewry Street and Southgate Street, where they cross the High Street near its northern end, the traffic struggles fitfully to cross the city via the "chicane" of traffic lights where all three roads intersect. The financial origins of Jewry Street have already been commented upon, while today it is a busy, bustling thoroughfare and because of the traffic it is not always possible to enjoy its rich variety of architectural styles. Nor is it possible to take in, at a glance, the opening up and closing of the spaces of the street or the subtle curving movement as it progresses from the High Street, through to the North Walls, marking the topmost boundary of the medieval city. Two notable buildings, namely the **Congregational Church** of 1853, now part embedded in the Old Gaol of 1805, will be dealt with in subsequent chapters. However, the **Library** on the west side of the street, now housed in the original Corn Exchange designed by the architect Owen Browne Carter in 1838, must be its

Offices of the Hampshire County Council Architect
The centrepiece of which is No. 77 High Street, a classical building with pilasters through three storeys, above deep rustications at ground floor level.

Royal Hampshire Regimental Museum
Serles House. *(Probably 1710-30.)*
"Stands back on its own, and is conceived in a surprising scale"(Pevsner/Lloyd)

St. Clement Street at its junction with St. Thomas Street
This is a street interconnected also with Southgate Street at the far end. It is a quiet enclave with a mixture of dwellings and shops and attractive smallness of scale.

The Library
The Library in Jewry Street was originally the Corn Exchange, designed by the Architect Owen Browne Carter in 1838

most significant and notable building. It is a robust classical building, with a projecting portico and columns beneath a fine pediment, surmounted by a central tower feature. Within its walls is housed the Local History Collection, administered by a most willing and helpful staff. Of particular interest are the Victorian Ordnance Survey Maps of the city. These maps give deep insight into city life at that time, together with its buildings and historic remains. The exactitude of detail harks back to an era of labour intensive surveying operations, a far cry from the modern and clinically exact "Superplans". This remark should not be construed as critical, but merely as an observation of the contrast between the Victorian and modern eras, with changed priorities, emphasis and outlook.

In Southgate Street the overall character is somewhat quieter than Jewry Street, with terraces of fine town houses and those of a smaller scale on its eastern side. Near the top end, **St. Clement Street** offers an intersection and cross-roads, reinforcing the domestic feeling of the street overall, with the seeming absence of the hurry and scurry of traffic seen elsewhere. St. Clement Street forms a link with the sequestered atmosphere of the Cathedral Close and College near at hand. On the western side of the street are two striking landmark buildings, namely the **Royal Hampshire Regimental Museum** cheek by jowl with the soaring spire of the **Church of St. Thomas and St. Clement**. The Museum stands well back from the road, in a dignified manner, with gardens and flags in front of the building dating from about 1710-20.

Moving now to the east side of the city, across the City Bridge and River Itchen, is **Chesil Street** running north-south and seen against the backdrop of St. Giles'

No.1 Chesil Street
This is the world famous Chesil Rectory, a 15th Century timber framed building, now serving as a restaurant.

Hill, also to the east. At No. **1 Chesil Street** is the world famous Chesil Rectory, a 16th. century timber framed building. The character of this road, because of its tight location between the river and the hill, is somewhat dark and almost foreboding, accentuated by the grimy facades of some of its buildings, for instance the **Church of St. Peter**, situated hard against the western side of the road. Notwithstanding this however, there is an overriding positive factor, that properties to the west side back on to and face the river, where there are some idyllic gardens sloping down to the river bank, with a myriad of features

and some beautiful old brick walls at the water's edge. This is the scene which presumably inspired Anthony Trollope to write – "*the banks of the little river, which flows nearby, round the Cathedral Close, being on the side furthest from the town.*" The river here has been a source of waterborne communication at various times in Winchester's history, and it is therefore, a fitting place to pause on this same topic.

Extract from the Ordnance Survey Map of 1871

This shows the Great Hall, (Castle Hall), and former Grand Jury Chambers, the lines of the Castle Ditch and the West Gate, all part of the original Castle and its fortifications. (Reproduced by courtesy of the Hampshire Local Studies Collection, County Library and the Ordnance Survey.)

Ecavations to the north of the Great Hall

Foundations of the "Round Tower" of 1222-3, and the "garderobe", the former being part of the Castle fortifications, and the latter evidence of the vital sanitary drainage system. The "sally-port" and "curtain" wall features are also shown and explained as part of the display.

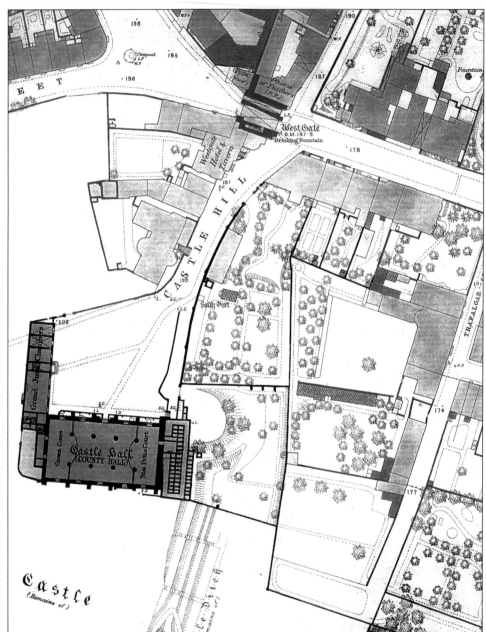

Chapter 4

WINCHESTER CASTLE AND THE GREAT HALL PRECINCT

The Castle at Winchester, for decades the administrative centre of Hampshire County Council, shares the site of the ancient Castle, dating from the time of William the Conqueror during his reign from 1066-1087. Upon the escarpment rising naturally from the level of present-day Southgate Street up to the line of the modern railway cutting, a great mound of earth was raised additionally, to form the platform on which this innovative fortification was to be built. From the early beginnings a wooden wall was built upon the earthen ramparts, a precursor to the stone fortifications typical of the post Norman era, but hitherto unknown in this country. Over the ensuing centuries these fortifications were to grow in sophistication and importance until their final demise when in 1651 on the order of Oliver Cromwell, the entire Castle was demolished. The only tangible evidence of this formidable Castle today, (apart from the mound on which it stood), is the **Great Hall** built in 1222-36; the east end of which was set against the City Wall, and excavations of the **Great Round Tower** constructed in 1222-3. These excavations can be seen at the end of Castle Avenue and to the north of the Great Hall.

The fortifications of the Castle were sited in a westerly direction beyond the city walls but attached thereto, and on a long tapering site. Beyond this and to the north was the **Westgate of the City**, interconnected to the Castle by a short run of the encircling **City Wall**. This wall protecting the city has been described as approximately 3.5 metres in width, in front of which was a great ditch said to be some 40 metres wide and 12 metres deep. This ditch also extended around all sides of the Castle and was called the "*Castle Ditch*". The original form of the Castle, in about 1067, was along traditional Norman lines, i.e. built on a "motte" or mound and defended by a rampart and ditch with some form of timber palisade (fence) and timber superstructure. During the reign of King Henry 1 (1100-1135), the timber defences were replaced by a square stone keep or stronghold, to secure royal treasures including the famous Domesday Book. Subsequently King Henry 11, (reigned 1154-89), added the **Royal Chapels and Apartments,** which further enlarged the castle. Unfortunately, during the reign of King John (reigned 1199-1216), the castle was besieged and severely damaged, but in the kingship of Henry 111 (reigned 1216-72), the castle was again enlarged and improved more on the lines of a palace. In 1222 the square Norman keep was demolished and replaced by a large round tower, the remains of which are seen in the excavations referred to above.

In all, the castle had eight towers throughout its history including the "new" **Round Tower** of 1222-3. This tower was most sophisticated in design, including the sally-port features which were underground passages connecting both the inner and outer fortifications and the other towers. In other words, it would be possible to use the passages to move around in safety and regroup with the ebb and flow of battle, quite out of sight of the enemy. Other features

The Great Hall
View looking east showing the ornate pair of stainless steel gates, designed by Antony Robinson of Shrewsbury in 1983, to commemorate the marriage in 1981 of the Prince and Princess of Wales.

such as a "*garderobe*", a euphemism for a toilet in a medieval castle, projecting beyond the wall and draining into the moat, as well as a "*postern gate*", a concealed entrance at the back of the castle, are evident today in the excavations on the Castle site. The remaining towers were the North West Tower, the Tower behind the Hall (1252-56), the King's Chapel Tower (1241-46), St. Catherine's Tower (1249-52), the Tower above the Prison (1258), the South West Tower, and the Jew's Tower. Overall at its zenith the Castle comprised the Barbican Ditch, Bridge and Gate-house, (on the north west- side), Curtain Wall, Great Hall, Great Chapel, 12th century Keep, Outer and Inner Bailey, (defended inner spaces), the City Wall and the West Gate. Infrastructure elements like the garderobe have already been referred to but facilities for the garrison would have included water supplies from wells as well as food storage facilities plus living quarters for the troops and stabling for the horses. There was even an herb garden, essential in medieval times for both medicine as well as cooking.

Today the Great Hall built between 1222-36 makes a splendid climax to the vista from the Westgate. This view is now framed by the Hampshire County Council Offices, on either side of Castle Avenue, following developments, which took place at the turn of the 20th century. Historically the approach to "Castle Hall", as it was once called, had been via Castle Hill, inside the City Wall, as seen on the Ordnance Survey Map of 1871. At that time "County Hall" as it was also called, was host to both the Crown and Nisi Prius Courts, with the Grand Jury Chamber at right angles to the main building and facing Castle Yard. Today there is an interesting cluster of buildings, other than the Great Hall, namely **Castle Hill Offices** built in 1894-5, and **Castle Avenue Offices** erected in 1912 and 1932.

The Great Hall
This picture of the Great Hall show its relationship with both Castle Hill offices to the left and Castle Avenue offices to the right.

The Castle Hill Offices, designed by James Robinson and Sir Arthur Blomfield, are in a flamboyant Tudor style, with flint walls and stone dressings to both doors and bay windows; together with soaring stone chimneys and a fine turret feature topped by a copper cupola. The Castle Avenue Offices, designed by Sir T.G. Jackson and Sir Herbert Baker respectively, are in a more sober and restrained style reminiscent of the Elizabethan era. At the far end, in Castle Yard and at right angles and attached to the Great Hall, is a link with the Castle Avenue Offices dating from 1774, designed by the surveyor Thomas Whitcombe. This is the building referred to above as the Grand Jury Room, now entered by a short flight of stone steps and leading to the present Public Entrance to the Great Hall via some splendid exhibition spaces.

The first interior view of the **Great Hall**, "*considered by many to be the finest medieval hall in England, after Westminster.*" Its internal volume is thought to be based on

The Round Table in the Great Hall
View looking looking west at the renowned "Round Table" dating from 1250-80, relating to the legend of King Arthur.

a double cube i.e. 33.5 metres x 16.75 metres x 2, and was constructed and conceived by the mason called Stephen. This great room is entered looking east, towards the ornate pair of stainless steel gates sculpted by Antony Robinson, to commemorate the wedding of HRH The Prince of Wales to Lady Diana Spencer in July 1981. The paintings on the east wall dating from 1874 records the County's parliamentary representatives from the time of Edward 1 (reigned 1272-1307), while the gates lead to the adjoining **Law Courts** opened in 1974. The dominant feature of this room however is the beautiful and lofty ceiling of intricate timber roof trusses. Below this are the elegant Purbeck Marble column shafts supporting the Early English Gothic stone pointed arches, over the five bays of this building. The Gothic windows are thought to be among the finest examples of 13th century design and craftsmanship. The west gable window shows three kings represented i.e. Arthur, Alfred and Canute, while in the eastern gable window William 1, Stephen and Henry 11 are seen. Looking to the west there is the famous **Round Table**, dating from 1250-80, attached to the stone wall, relating to the legend of King Arthur. In the centre of this table is the "Tudor Rose" motive, and the radiating pattern of green and white, the colours of the Tudor dynasty. Below this table once stood the Judge's bench, now seen against the north wall of the hall. The room is illuminated by elegant Early English Gothic stone windows with "*plate tracery*" and a quatrefoil motive set in the apex of the pointed stone arches above. Over the centuries this great room has been the scene of many legal trials, perhaps the most notorious being that of Dame Alice Lisle, condemned to death by Judge Jeffereys in 1685, after having been found not guilty at her first trial for harbouring those fleeing the Monmouth rebellion! In more modern times **Alfred Thomson Denning**. (Baron Denning of Whitchurch), frequently sat here in judgement, best known for his humanity and fairness. The last time the court sat in session here was in 1973, for the trial of the Price sisters convicted at that time for IRA terrorism.

One curious feature of this room which cannot be overlooked, and tucked away in the in the south west corner, is the large bronze statue of Queen Victoria (reigned 1837-1901), by the sculptor Sir Alfred Gilbert, who was also responsible for the Eros Statue in Piccadilly Circus in London. This statue is unique that it is the only one of the

"Tower - Gatehouse, Winchester 1828"
Print of an engraving of the West Gate, (West Side), dated 1828 and entitled "Tower Gatehouse Winchester".
The original central arch and pedestrian way to the left can be clearly seen, the latter feature dating from 1791, prior to which this same space was occupied by the Porter's Lodge. (Author's Collection.)

East View of the King's House, and the adjoining Offices, as Intended to have been finish'd by Sir Christopher Wren.

West View of the Ancient Castle of Winchester.

East View of the Ancient Castle of Winchester.

Published as the Act directs Nov.1.1798. by Ja.s Robbins Winchester.

Print of engravings of the King's House

*East View of the King's House and adjoining Offices, as intended
to be finished by Sir Christopher Wren. (Reproduced by courtesy of
the Hampshire Record Office.)*

The old Military Barracks
These apartments, now occupying the old Military Barracks, retain the grandeur and pomp of the original Victorian Buildings.

few in which the Queen is depicted as seated. The sculpture was first unveiled in Castle Yard in 1887 by Princess Louise, daughter of Queen Victoria; although later dismantled in 1892 and re-sited in Abbey Gardens, beside the Guildhall, and in 1910 was brought to the Great Hall, where it has remained since occupying several positions.

Externally the walls of the Great Hall are faced with a combination of flint and cream coloured random stones, which together give off a strange luminous aura. This combines with a seemingly "freckled" appearance arising from the ad hoc arrangement of the masonry. However the overall effect on its character is one of robustness and strength, reinforced by the powerful buttresses and the seemingly "solid" porch on the north elevation. The cobbled forecourt and natural stone paving elsewhere hark back in character to its medieval origins as part of a formidable and famous fortress and royal residence.

The **Westgate** is essentially 13th century in origin although its west face, (i.e. outside the City Wall), is of the

14th century. Strategically it is considered as part of the Castle fortifications, by virtue of its link via the ramparts of the City Wall, giving access to the Round Tower with its postern gate on its inner city side. It was through its central arch that entrance to the city was gained, and this continued until 1959, when traffic was diverted around its north side. The pedestrian way to the north of the gate dates from 1791, although prior to this the Porter's Lodge occupied this space. Currently, access to the upper chamber above the central arch, (now a museum), is via a long flight of irregular stone steps. At the foot of these stairs is the location of a small chamber, which once served as a jailhouse until 1760. The general plan arrangement of the Westgate is seen on the 1871 Ordnance Survey Map, although access to the upper chamber at that time was by a dogleg staircase entered from the central arch.

Apart from its defensive and security role the Westgate was also an administrative centre, regulating the ebb and flow of commerce in and away from the city, and tolls and duties were collected here by officials, assisted by the porter. (Nearby there was a great weighing machine in the street now called Staple Gardens used for this purpose.) In the 18th century, part of the gatehouse was used as an extension to the "**Plume of Feathers**" public house. Immediately adjacent and to the north, one of the city's churches was sited, aptly named "**St. Mary Outside Westgate**", although now no longer present in the street scene. In an engraving of 1828 entitled "Tower Gatehouse Winchester", the 14th century west front can be clearly seen, with both the central arch and north passage, and with buildings hard against the north and south faces, all details of which are confirmed in the later map of 1871 referred to above.

Through the central arch looking to the east, there is a sequential view of the city into the High Street, past the

***East View of King's House
at Winchester***
*Engraving of 1830 i.e. before
the great fire of 1894. These
details coincide with a
photograph of the remains of
the King's House after the fire.
New Barracks were built on
the same site in 1899,
conserving some of the remains
of the previous buildings.
(Author's Collection.)*

Buttercross and with a distant perspective of St. Giles' Hill. There is a cobbled pedestrian access beneath the pointed arch of the Westgate, over which are two slit windows with circular gunports at each base. Immediately above are two emblazoned shields with a cluster of stone gargoyles around. At the highest level are machicolations, being projections at parapet level, with openings below through which missiles could be dropped on the enemy. Beneath the arches, both west and east, are stone and flint walls while above a timber beamed ceiling is seen in the half-light. Around the outer and inner arches are slots for both a portcullis and defensive doors, long since removed as redundant! The principal role of the porter was to ensure that these gates were closed at curfew each day and opened

in the morning. At curfew time all citizens were required to put out their fires for reasons of communal safety, (timber framed buildings were a primary fire hazard), the closed city gave peace of mind and security to the population, and law and order could best be maintained.

Leaving the Westgate and moving along Romsey Road for a short distance, the entrance to the **Peninsula Barracks** comes into view on the left. These Barracks are currently home to the Royal Green Jackets Museum, the Gurkha Museum and the Royal Hussars Museum. Around the now deserted parade grounds, the original barrack buildings are home to modern apartments by conversion, the army having moved out. It was on this site however that the parameters of Winchester Castle were drawn, and significantly at a later date that **Sir Christopher Wren** drew up grand plans for a Palace here for King Charles 11, begun in 1683 and stopped in 1685 with the King's death. Two fine engravings exist showing firstly *"The East View of the King's House"* which interestingly also includes a western panoramic view of Winchester Castle. The second engraving is also a view of that part of the Palace which was actually built and is captioned *"Engraving from a drawing taken on the spot by an officer"*. These images are the only concrete evidence of the appearance of the buildings, which were engulfed by a major fire in 1894. The fire occurred on the 19th of December in that year, starting at 12.16 a.m., and described in official records as *" the most dangerous and disastrous fire the Brigade has ever been called upon to attend"*. Be that as it may, this truly was a remarkable building. Fortunately, records actually exist in the form of drawings and a "Memorandum Book" giving details of the financial estimates for the contract and instructions for payment in respect of the laying of the foundation stone on the 23 rd March 1683. (At that date Wren was 51 years of age.)

Today the site of the Castle exudes an aura of timelessness and a profound sense of history. The great pool, which now sparkles in the sunlight in front of the new apartment blocks, reflects images of the grandeur and pomp of the ornate Victorian buildings which continue in spirit the ancient military tradition of the barracks and most grand, Winchester Castle.

**Engraving of Bishop
William of Wykeham**
*An assumed likeness taken
from an original engraving
entitled "After the Portrait in
St. Mary's College Winchester
and the Monumental Effigy in
Winchester Cathedral".
Published in 1860, in
B.B. Woodward's "A History of
Winchester" (Author's
Collection).*

Chapter 5

WINCHESTER COLLEGE

The history of Winchester College is inextricably linked with the name of its founder **Bishop William of Wykeham**, a man born of humble parentage, but who rose to the highest of offices both in the State and ultimately within the Church. It is recorded that he was responsible for purchasing the land for the College in 1382, and masterminding the planning and construction of the collegiate complex prior to its opening in 1394, when the first intake of "scholars" took place.

Any first visitor to the College will be impressed by the bastion-like appearance of the formidable flint walls of the College Street façade. The reason for this harks back to the need for security, at a time of social unrest with the terrors of the Peasants Revolt of 1381 still fresh then in everyone's mind. Add to this the fact that the College was sited just outside the relative safety of the City Walls, the need was even greater to ensure the safety of the scholars and those who were to teach them. Once through the gateway at the Porter's Lodge, the sequence of buildings arranged around courtyards only adds to the feeling of a sequestered, safe and almost womblike character.

What then was the raison d'etre for the building of this College, and what rationale inspired the administration of what is claimed to be the first of England's Public Schools? To answer these questions it is important to understand further the historical background of the times of its foundation as well as the motives and psyche of its founder.

To begin with the **Black Death of 1348-49** and its decimation of part of the population had resulted in a paucity of academic standards of the men presenting themselves for the "ministry". It was this shortfall that William sought to address by the opening of this centre of high academic training at Winchester. One must remember also the lowly origins of this man born in the year 1312, to parents living in a small cottage in the Hampshire village of Wickham. Although he received a "grammar school" education in Winchester he left school to become notary to the Constable of Winchester, thereby losing out on a university education. Notwithstanding this apparent setback, he went on to rise through the ranks, as it were, firstly as King's Clerk and Surveyor at Windsor Castle where he had fortuitously come into contact with William Wynford, master mason (who William was later to commission to carry out the remodelling works in the Nave of Winchester Cathedral). On June 12th 1362 he was ordained priest and in 1364 King Edward 111(reigned 1327-77) appointed him Private Secretary and Keeper of the Privy Seal. Finally, in 1366 William became Bishop of Winchester and Chancellor of England.

It has been suggested that as with all his building works at Winchester, the founding and construction of this College was above all an act of piety. In addition it was a manifestation of an inner desire for an earthly monument to perpetuate his name, more potent than his shrine in the Cathedral. Be that as it may, he certainly was a man of great energy, vision and strength of character, borne out by his striking portrait in St. Mary's College. However, the founding of this College was a departure from the norm in the way the educational system there was organised. In the first place the governance of the College was carried out in accordance and strict conformity with the statutes as laid down by the founder. Originally there was a Warden, with 70 scholars, 10 priests as fellows, 3 chaplains, 3 clerks, 16 choristers (quiristers), a Schoolmaster called "*Informator*", and an Under-master called "*Hostiarius*". The scholars were chosen by examination and according to Bernard Woodward, in his "History of Winchester" published in 1860, only admissible after passing a test "*differing in difficulty for candidates between ten and twelve, and those between twelve and fourteen*".

The real departure in the case of Winchester College from that of contemporary institutions was that it was independent from other seats of learning, and unlike earlier grammar schools, for instance Winchester Grammar School, was not an appendage of a monastic or collegiate foundation. In other words the "**Seinte Marie College of Wynchestre**" was both independent and self governing, with internal discipline effected by the boys themselves by the presence of school prefects. Initially the scholars received their education free, but eventually a new breed of paying pupils called "commoners", i.e. *commensales,* were admitted, for whom between 1724-66 the then headmaster Dr. John Burton built living accommodation called "commons", hence their name. In essence this arrangement persists to this day, although numerically the original intake of 10 commoners has risen to some 600 now arranged within 10 houses. These houses, named Bramston's, Chernocke House, Du Boulay's, Fearon's, Hawkins', Kingsgate House, Moberley's, Morshead's,

The Outer Gate
A carved figurehead in the ceiling vaults, who appears to smile on those entering the College and to scowl on their leaving.

Sergeant's, and Turner's, are sited to the west of the College in Kingsgate Street and beyond.

The main entrance to the College is via the **Outer Gate** in College Street, which road is parallel to and outside the protection of the Cathedral Close walls. The gatehouse itself is in the form of a simple stone and flint faced two-storey tower with an octagonal staircase outside rising above roof level surmounted with crenellations. Apart from the central niche feature, with a stone statue of the Virgin and Child above the flat inclined stone arch of the entrance gates, the elevation is almost devoid of decoration. The severity of the original college architecture has already been commented upon, and the earlier experiences of Wykeham and master mason William Wynford at Windsor Castle are here clearly evident in the *"bastion- like appearance"*. Beneath the arched entrance there is a simple cobblestone floor while above there is a beautiful lierne stone vault to surprise the eye of the first-time visitor. On a carved boss where the stone ribs of the vault intersect, is a carved figurehead who appears to smile on those entering the College and to scowl when leaving!

Immediately to the left of the 14th century Outer Gate are the **Warden's Lodgings**, also facing College Street and extending eastwards, first built by Warden John Harmar in 1597. It is here that the street scene begins to lighten, where flint walls and awesomely large stone buttresses give way to soft red brick walls above. These walls are now punctuated with painted sash windows on two floors set beneath timber modillioned cornices and a mellow plain tiled roof. The brick-arched windows were inserted later in about 1730 and demonstrate that with the passing of time the defensive facades have given way to a more relaxed appearance, albeit at a level well above the street. Beyond this is a long brick wall enclosing the Warden's garden and

Outer Gate to Winchester College
Behind this simple 14th Century arch is a vaulted ceiling above a cobble stone floor, leading to Outer Court. Beyond this are views of Middle Gate leading onwards to the inner courtyard, i.e. Chamber Court

Warden's Lodgings
View of the east side of the Warden's Lodgings from College Street, seen above the walls enclosing the majestic lawns of the Warden's Garden.

affording overviews of the remodelling of the Warden's Lodgings by Warden John Nicholas in 1692, and later by G.S. Repton in 1832-3, urbanely presented in red brick walls and sash windows etc. throughout.

Returning to the entrance, to the right and the west is the old Brewhouse, which now functions as the College **Moberley Library** to designs by the architect Sir Herbert Baker in 1932-4. Again, the walls facing the street are flint faced with some of the original slit windows and some later interventions. In the pitched roof above there remains the old ventilator from the brewing days, and it is here that the eye is arrested by the soaring triple octagonal chimneys on the flank wall of the **Headmaster's House**, 19th century Gothic in style, built in the period 1839-42 to the designs of G.S. Repton. Architecturally this house is visually powerful and assertive and creates a dominant articulation in the street at a point where there is an immediate change of mood and softness, with the coloured façade of the house famous as the last residence of the novelist Jane Austen,

who is now buried in the north aisle of the Cathedral.

Returning once more to the College entrance, and passing the Porter's Lodge, the **Outer Court** is found. In this place once stood the working areas of the College complex, where in addition to the brewery, there was a bake-house and granary on land now occupied by the Warden's Lodging. Other facilities existed like stables and a slaughterhouse well hidden from view. In other words, the College was designed to be self sufficient in line with arrangements of the day. Today, as before, this space is dominated by **Middle Gate** (leading to Chamber Court), where originally the Warden lived, affording a good view of all that came and went. The walls of the surrounding buildings are flint faced, this time in a more regular pattern than those facing the road outside. Again the windows are severe and lancet-like and barred, thereby perpetuating the fortified image of the College, so far.

Next to this space and through a further archway **Chamber Court** comes into view. This in effect is the nerve

Chamber Court
"The centre of College life", according to "Notions" the Official Winchester College Handbook. Built in 1387-94, little has changed in its appearance while Middle Gate, seen on the north side, contains rooms where once the Warden lived.

Chapel
The 15th century, Perpendicular Gothic Bell Tower, built in 1488 and rebuilt in 1863, dominates the skyline of the College, and acts as a visual foil to the similarly lofty and elegant windows which illuminate the interior of the main body of Chapel.

centre of the College and was built in 1387-94. Here there is a change of architectural emphasis and drama. The walls of flint give way to dressed stone in the Chapel situated in the south-east of the courtyard and Hall, together with Seventh Chamber in the south-west. It is here also that the buildings show true finesse and style commensurate with the importance of their function.

The points of entry to these three buildings are found in the south-west corner and in reverse order **Seventh Chamber** is entered from Chamber Passage from a single oak door opened by an enormous iron key. Once inside this schoolroom, said to be the oldest in England, the space is occupied by tiers of timber walled study cubicles called *"toys"* on two levels. The atmosphere is both timeless and

monastic, reminiscent of niches in a cloister where a monk might sit and read. The stone walls are lit by Gothic tracery and adorned by many inscribed plaques. Above this room is **Hall** approached by a long flight of wooden steps in the courtyard adjacent to Chamber Passage, and at the head of these stairs is the world famous painting of the "Trusty Servant". (A portrait by the artist William Cave, depicting the attributes of the ideal servant, in rather tongue-in-cheek terms). Hall is an imposing room, in which are arranged long wooden dining tables together with square *"plates"* called *"trenchers"* on which food is served, hence the origin of the expression *"a square meal"*! The panelling around the walls dates from 1540 and above this are portrait paintings including one of William of Wykeham in an assumed likeness. Elegant Gothic windows light this lofty room, some 12.2 metres high, and the roof itself is low pitched with arched braces. Because of the elevated siting of this room security again comes to mind and is confirmed by a large transverse oak beam, which slides into a recess of the stone walls, to bar the door leading to the stairs. Even the salt was kept in a small octagonal chest, secured by a lock. The only means of unimpeded access and entry was by means of a small medieval "cat flap", leading into a turret staircase on the other side of the room.

Beyond the end wall of Hall is **Chapel** which, rising to the two levels of Hall and Seventh Chamber combined, is visually divided outside by the soaring **Bell-Tower**, attached to the south side. An ante chapel situated beneath the end bay of Hall enters Chapel from Chamber Court, this ante chapel being divided from the main chapel by a stone screen. Although Chapel is medieval in origin, the architect William Butterfield restored it in the 19th century and re-built the tower. Consequently according to Notions *"only the walls, roof, and the Dons' seats behind the Choir are original"*. (Notions is a small blue handbook being in part a dictionary of the Wykehamist's private language). The roof of Chapel is quite spectacular, with fan vaulting in red and gold painted ribs with a plain field behind. However the vaulting is constructed in timber throughout, in a manner to simulate stone. The use of timber was a device to reduce the weight of the superstructure on the walls and foundations. Like the Cathedral nearby, there were foundation problems associated with building on marshy ground. Originally some very fine wood panelling in carved oak adorned Chapel, by the woodcarver Edward Pierce. This panelling was subsequently removed, and in part has now found a new home in the contemporary building of New Hall.

Cloisters
These beautiful Cloisters, built in the Perpendicular Gothic style, and open to the elements on one side, originally arranged for study in true monastic fashion, gives credence to the name for Summer Term i.e. "Cloister Time" because of the tradition of teaching here during the summer.

Thurbern's Chantry was built as an addition to Chapel in 1473-85, but in 1862-3 was completely rebuilt on the advice of William Butterfield. This small building of just two bays, with its lierne-vaulted roof and decorative

School
*Built in 1683-7 by Warden John Nicholas at a cost of £2600.00,
designed in the style of Wren, but not attributable to him by
documentary evidence. (Sir Christopher Wren, 1632-1723,
worked in Winchester designing the so called King's House for
King Charles 11, from 1683-5 when, quite coincidentally, the
construction of School was in progress at the same time!).*

Moberly's
*Entrance to Moberly's, (from Kingsgate Street), a Commoner
House founded in 1860 but situated within a building
comprising 68-70 Kingsgate Street dating from 1571.*

bosses, was erected to commemorate Warden Thurbern, who died in 1450. This Chantry stands cheek by jowl with the Bell-Tower, which built in the Perpendicular Gothic style, dominates the skyline of the College.

Immediately to the south of Chapel are **Cloisters** some 40 metres square on plan, and built at an odd angle to the adjoining complex. Within the centre space of Cloisters is **Fromond's Chantry**, which was built in 1420. Facing the courtyard these cloisters are open to the elements, and here display some fine Perpendicular Gothic style open tracery, below which are placed stone seats. Above there is a beautifully elegant roof of arched timber rafters, and below this a floor of rich red-brown clay tiles. There has been some previous structural movement here,

with stonework out of the perpendicular, but this just adds to the authenticity and charm. It is thought that the stone seats were originally arranged for study, in true monastic fashion. This is confirmed by the tradition of teaching here during the warmer weather, hence to this day Summer Term is called *"Cloister Time"*.

Immediately adjacent and to the west is **School** built in 1683-7, to compensate for overcrowding in Seventh Chamber as the number of *"day boys"* had swelled the ranks

Art School
Edward Cullinan's design for the Art School, as seen from
Kingsgate Street, blending the old with the new, in a manner both
whimsical and full of serious intent. There is a vision panel, in
the door to the life room shaped like a keyhole, with a metal flap
for modesty!

73

of scholars. This is an extremely handsome building of red brick with stone window surrounds, plinth and quoins. It is exactly symmetrical, and entered by a central doorway on the north side, surmounted by a pediment feature at roof level, below which is a carved figure of William of Wykeham, sculpted by C.G. Cibber in 1692. School is a complete departure both in style and the way the building is sited, standing alone and unprotected by a surrounding wall. There have been many debates as to whether this building was designed by Sir Christopher Wren, while he was engaged with his scheme for the King's Palace in Winchester. Although School is not documented in "*Parentalia*" it certainly has the attributes of the master's work, in the decorative use of stonework against a brick background. In the south and west wings of Hampton Court Palace, Wren anglicised classical design using brick as opposed to stone for the walls, employing stone to highlight the elegance of the proportions of each element in the design. Whether or not Wren designed School it is certainly in his style.

At the time of writing School was being refurbished and inside new floors and wall panelling were self-evident The overall impact of the interior is of a unified space brought about by the double cube proportions of this splendid room. Modern tables and chairs are in contrast with the original throne-like Headmaster's Chair with the Second Master's Chair opposite. At the outset the room was designed to accommodate four classes with a central study, which nestled around a large fireplace. Today portraits bedeck the walls above the fine wood panelling with figures now arranged looking to the centre of this unified space. Above all this is a beautiful pargetted and coved plaster ceiling adorned further with a brass chandelier of 1729. Opposite the entrance door there is an

Art School
The pristine entrance hall to the Art School, with its successful fusion of traditional and modern motifs.

interior middle timber pediment, against which are hung two Flemish tapestries. This little building is a one-off jewel in the crown of Winchester College!

Moving forward to Victorian times, (Victoria reigned 1837-1901), there was a major flurry of building activity with the founding of no less than ten Commoner Houses between 1859 and 1905. The first of these was **Chernocke House**, founded in 1859, now sited at the junction of St. Cross Road and Romans Road, and in a building designed by Sir Charles Nicholson in 1910-12. This is a sombre flint faced building, Gothic in style, and with an almost ecclesiastic character reminiscent of Nicholson's church work, culminating in his designs at St. Thomas's Cathedral in Portsmouth carried out in the 1930's. In the main the other houses are red brick, four storeys high, under slate roofs, apart from Moberly's in Kingsgate Street. These buildings represent a large extension to the original medieval complex of Wykeham's original College, and are all sited west of Kingsgate Street and the continuing Kingsgate Road. These College Houses were constructed to house the influx of commoners from the middle of the 19th Century. Today these Commoners can be seen streaming towards the **Commoner Gate** in Kingsgate Street, which gate was designed by Frank L. Pearson in 1902-4 as part of the memorial to the Wykehamists who fell in the South African War. Built in stone with Gothic turrets, in what has been described as ornate Perpendicular, it is strangely evocative but seemingly out of place in an otherwise sombre street.

However, once past the Commoner Gate, another war memorial comes into view, this time to the dead of the two World Wars, in the guise of the **War Cloister** designed by the architect Sir Herbert Baker in 1922-4. Arranged around an open courtyard in the Classical style, there are semicircular stone arches, with circular Hopton Stone columns supporting the Cotswold Stone vaulting. Here the walls are mainly in flint with a stone frieze inscription leading the eye around the walkway at a higher level, while a cool stone floor completes the scene. This building is a complete departure in design terms from the main College complex, even the way the flint walls are treated represents a change in character with insets of stone and other coloured and decorative devices. Atmospherically it is serene as befits its function, but it is more Italian than English in its effect.

There are too many buildings to mention individually within the two main complexes sited generally to the east and west of the Kingsgate Street environs. However two relatively modern buildings come to mind in conclusion, namely **New Hall** designed by the architect Sir Peter Shepheard in 1958-60 in the south of the Warden's Garden, and the **Art School** to the designs of Edward Cullinan more recently. Both buildings are a metamorphosis of both tradition and modernity. The former is notable for assimilating the florid wood panelling from the Chapel around its walls, the latter for conceiving new uses for a redundant building and at the same time creating a contemporary environment for the arts.

Finally there are some splendid open spaces forming the backdrop to the College namely Meads, New Field, Gater Field, and Palmer Field, all close to the River Itchen, which flows serenely by. Within these spaces are some little gems of architecture such as the Mill near to New Hall. An atmosphere of tradition and timelessness pervades the air, but there is also a strong sense of new ideas and progress towards a new century symbolised by the creativity of this place where "Manners Mayketh Man".

Engraving 1838
*St Cross Church, from the north east as seen from the River
Itchen and the water meadows, once praised for"its stately outline
which crowns the watery glade", (The Times early 19th century,
Author's Collection).*

Chapter 6

THE HOSPITAL OF ST. CROSS
AND ST. CROSS CHURCH

Approaching Winchester from the south, along the old Roman road leading from the village of Compton, the Hospital of St. Cross and its church nestles alongside the River Itchen, and is seen against the backdrop of the water meadows, while the square Norman tower of St. Cross Church is the first visible landmark from the road, signifying the discreet presence of this venerable institution.

St. Cross Hospital was founded in 1136 by Henry de Blois, Bishop of Winchester, and grandson of King William 1 (the Conqueror). St. Cross began as, and remains, a charitable institution, originally intended to support, "*thirteen poor and impotent men, so reduced in strength as rarely or never able to raise themselves without the assistance of another*", who, when they had recovered their strength be "*dismissed with decency and respect*". In addition, provision was also made at that time for "*a hundred other poor men of good conduct*" to be fed at dinner while assistance was to be given "*according to the means of the house, to the needy of every description*". In other words it was to be a microcosm of the Welfare State in medieval England, at a time of general hardship to the poor.

The **Anglo-Saxon Chronicles** for the year 1137 refer to the harshness of the reign of King Stephen (1135-54), "*never was there such wretchedness in the land*". Throughout his 19-year rule of oppression, towns were obliged to pay a tax called "tenser", a form of protection money, and when there was no more money to give, land and buildings were plundered and burnt. The chroniclers continue by saying,

"*whenever the land was tilled, the earth bore no corn, for the land was ruined by such deeds*". It is therefore against this social background that the true worth and need for the foundation of St. Cross should be judged today.

The foundation of the Hospital of St. Cross was funded by the tithes from 15 churches in Hampshire, Oxfordshire and Wiltshire, although its early history was marred by financial mismanagement. For instance, in 1151 Bishop de Blois assigned the management of the Hospital to the Knights Hospitallers of St. John of Jerusalem, an organisation for the protection of routes of pilgrimage to the Holy Land. However it was later found that funds intended for the Hospital went elsewhere, diminishing the charitable work, and holding up progress on the buildings. Over a period of 700 years subsequently, the Bishop of Winchester appointed Masters of St. Cross Hospital, but this did not stop the occasional wrongdoing. Matters in this respect came to a head when in 1808 the Reverend Francis North was appointed to the post of Master and thereafter was thought to have misappropriated funds to such an extent that the Hospital was all but ruined. Such was the publicity of the case that the matter was alluded to in "The Warden"; a novel by Anthony Trollope published in 1855. However the name of the establishment was changed to Hiram's Hospital, because as the author states "*we are anxious that no personality may be suspected*". As a result the management of St. Cross Hospital was reformed in 1855 and became governed by a Board of Trustees, which

Engraving 1780
View of the Inner Quadrangle looking towards the Beaufort Tower and Brethren's Hall, with the Brother's Quarters on the left and the west end of St. Cross Church on the right (Author's Collection).

continues to the present day.

The architecture of St. Cross Hospital is remarkable for the unity of its collegiate plan. Arranged around its two "Quadrangles", the Outer Quadrangle being small and intimate, leading beneath the arch of the 15th century Beaufort Tower to the open space of the Inner Quadrangle, the end vista of which is dominated by the fine cruciform late Norman Church. Within this quadrangle are the world famous Brothers' quarters, Master's Office, and 14th century Brethren's Hall.

Returning to the Outer Quadrangle, and moving from north to south, the entrance to the whole complex is via the 16th century Outer Gate, leading to the cobbled surface of the Outer Quadrangle. Inside is the 14th century Kitchen on the west, and on the other side the Old

Brewhouse and site of the former Hundred Men's Hall (alluding to the dining space of the "hundred other poor men of good conduct"). In the south-east corner is the Porter's Lodge, from where the *"Wayfarer's Dole"* traditionally comprising *"a morsel of bread and a horn of beer"* is given to visitors on request, harking back to the days when travellers were refreshed and thereby given respite, from often long and arduous journeys.

The stone and flint walls of the **Beaufort Tower** rise through three stages, and on its south-west corner, and facing the Inner Quadrangle, is the octagonal turret staircase rising to a higher level surmounted by its weathervane. This building was formerly part of the Master's Lodging, with the large window strategically placed at first-floor level to oversee the coming and going

View of St. Cross from the Water Meadows
This collegiate image of both the Church and administrative
buildings nestling within the enclosing walls bears witness to a
medieval institution, still in use for the original purpose of its
founders, as a haven for the poor and needy.

of visitors. The Madonna and Child motif in stone sculpture appears at second-floor level, and together with what can best be described as the "security window" on the first floor bears a striking similarity with the Entrance Gate and Warden's Lodging arrangements at Winchester College. From this former Master's Lodging there stretches a long two-storey ambulatory, or cloister, above which was the original infirmary, all on the east side of the Inner Quadrangle. On the cloister or ground floor level the construction is partly stone and flint with red brick lacing courses, together with open Tudor style timber arches, above which is a more solid arrangement of timber framing and plaster panels. In the centre of all this is a remarkable looking feature combining twin brick arches, beneath four small lancet windows, and at high level a plaque inscribed with the name of Henry Compton D.D.,

Master of St. Cross from 1667-75.

Immediately to the east of the Ambulatory is the Master's Garden, resplendent with lawn, pond and a magnificent plane tree. Around this garden is a great mellow brick and stone wall with its saddleback brick coping. This walled garden has been the Master's Garden since at least the 14th century, and the pond, (a fish-pond in fact), and dovecote provided a source of food in the Middle Ages, and served as a ready made larder. Alongside the Master's Garden is the so-called Compton Garden, containing botanical specimens from the "New World", created originally by William Compton who went on also to create the Gardens of Fulham Palace, while Bishop of London, when the Diocese of London included America! Turning now to the **Church of St. Cross**, the visual centrepiece of the whole complex, it is dedicated in honour

"Birds Beak" Window in the North Transept

This semi-circular arched window in the north transept is set within two bands of intricate carved images incorporating a continuous bird motif defined as a "beak head moulding".

St. Cross Church

View from the nave looking east, with the tower crossing and chancel beyond; a near perfect example of a Norman Early-English transitional church.

of the Holy Cross, being built originally in its first phase by Bishop Henry de Blois, so that *"the Brother's poor in Christ could humbly and devoutly worship God"*. The church was built in stages or "campaigns" as they are described in the Church Guide, over a period of some 200 years from about A.D. 1160-1340. Some biographical background to Bishop Henry has already been covered in Chapter 2, but suffice to say he was a truly remarkable man. Because of his immense wealth, and early training at Cluny, was able to be both a patron and innovator of architecture. It therefore comes as no surprise, that from his vision, the undisputed excellence of the Church of St. Cross has been handed down to this generation.

The plan of **St. Cross Church** is compact and cruciform, comprising a chancel at the east, with a central crossing beneath the tower, north and south transepts, the latter element with its sacristy, nave and side aisles, together with a north facing porch. As previously stated, the church is interconnected with the other hospital buildings by the ambulatory link, travelling north to south. Externally the plan form is resolved in a powerful architectural composition around the robust central tower, with its walls constructed in flint, (from the chalk downs), with stone dressings around the windows and doors. Stylistically it is a truly transitional building, a reflection of its gestation period of 200 years. The building began at the east chancel and it is here that the Norman influences dominate in the detailing. As observed by Pevsner/Lloyd in the Hampshire volume of the Buildings of England, on the issue of styles in this church, *"It is a matter of transition indeed, and a disorderly, illogical transition in which fully Gothic and truly Romanesque elements overlap"*. However, the ambiguities are all part of the charm of this building in which one architectural element merges gracefully into the next

without effort or excuse.

The entrance to the church is via the north porch, and the style here is distinctly Early English Gothic of the 13th century, with pointed lancet arched doorways, and a simple stone cross vault within the porch space. This porch marks the demarcation point within the nave beyond where the 13th century part gives way to the 12th century section towards the tower crossing and beyond. Inside, the height of the nave is almost overwhelming in its relationship with the shortness of the three-bay arcade, provoking a comment from the last century that it is *"remarkably lofty for its other proportions"*. What is even more remarkable is the design of the nave arcading with its circular Normanesque columns and capitals and the pointed Gothic arches above. At high level in the clerestorey windows there is a further change in style, with the progression of time in the building programme, giving way to the Decorated Gothic of the 14th century. The window tracery design and the formation of the stone ribs and vaulting further demonstrate this change over the nave. Below this is a beautiful encaustic tiled floor with a combination of red and grey tiles in a geometrical pattern which, combined further with tiles in yellow ochre, gives a distinctly Victorian aura of richness. (The architect William Butterfield had a hand in restoration works in the church during the years 1864-5.) In the south-west corner of the nave is a font taken from St. Faith's Church, since following its demolition in 1507, the parishioners were given the use of St. Cross Church in perpetuity as recompense for the loss of their church. (Currently the church notice board refers to "The Hospital of St. Cross Parish of St. Faith".)

The north and south transepts, together with the large and vertical space of the tower crossing, are of particular

The North Porch
This 13th century Early English Gothic porch, with its rib and panel vault, and pointed arch doorways, leads into the north side of the nave.

interest leading as they do to the chancel, the primary visual and religious focus of the church. Within the north transept there is the unique and extremely beautiful "Bird's Beak Window", set within two patterns of intricate Norman carved motifs incorporating a continuous bird motif defined as "beakhead", interwoven with the chevron work. All this artistry leads the eye towards the stained glass window, deep in the recess of masonry wall, and therein is displayed the text *By Thy Cross and Passion Good Lord deliver us*". On the north wall of this transept there are two interconnecting doors to the ambulatory, one at first-floor level together with an original 12th century door at ground level giving public access to the church. Strangely, however, the door at the upper level leads to a short flight of stone steps downward, to where there was once perhaps an intermediate floor or landing, but where there is now just an open space!

The **Lady Chapel**, entered from the south aisle of the church, is a place of exquisite beauty. There is a profusion of stone carving to be seen within this small space, both in the semicircular Norman style windows and unusually in the ribs of the vaulting, also seen elsewhere in the nave aisles. Above the altar is the further adornment of a Flemish triptych, of circa 1520, and a Jacobean altar rail. The richness of decoration and detail is in contrast with the plain stone walls. As elsewhere in this building the decorative tile floor gives colour and friendly warmth. The **North Chancel Chapel** is by contrast a more simple space, with the remains of some 13th century wall paintings of figures between stone arcading, all part of the first bay of the parclose screen separating the chapel from the chancel. There is a poignant memorial in this chapel to one Captain Russell, killed in action in the First World War, just a simple timber cross with the date 17-10-1916.

The Lady Chapel
The Lady Chapel, entered from the south transept is a quiet place of exquisite beauty, with the profusion of carving and adornment seen in the ribbed arches to the vaulting and around the windows.

The Brother's Quarters
*These quarters, sited on the west side of the Inner Quadrangle,
provide sheltered accommodation for some 25 men within the
striking architecture of flint walls with tiny leaded windows,
steeply sloping tiled roofs, and the whole punctuated by a rhythm
of "spectacular" chimney pieces.*

At the crossing, beneath the Norman tower, and at high level there is an ornate painted timber ceiling of blue, red and silver; all supported on corbels of carved stone faces. There are great vertical windows here in the Decorated Gothic style, accounted for chronologically by the rebuilding of the tower in 1384, when at the same time the re-roofing of the chancel took place. Architecturally the chancel is just two bays in length, in comparison with the nave and side aisles of three bays. An interesting observation about the style of this church overall is made in Bernard Woodward's History of Winchester published in the 1860's, when he records the following analysis. "*As far as the original work remains, the choir (i.e. Chancel), is Romanesque or Transitional Norman, with the pointed arch introduced as an arch of construction throughout, while the semi-circular form is retained as an arch of decoration.*" This explanation is by far the most rational and convincing argument to explain the aesthetic presentation of not only the chancel but also the whole church.

Leaving the church by the north porch, the visitor is now confronted by the **Brothers' Quarters** on the west side of the Inner Quadrangle, providing sheltered accommodation for some 25 men, comprising 17 of the original Order and up to 8 Brothers of the "Order of Noble Poverty". This latter Order was introduced after its foundation by Cardinal Henry Beaufort, Bishop of Winchester, and in 1445 built another almshouse for former servants of the State, "*for those who once everything handsome had about them, but had suffered losses*". Today the Brothers' Quarters comprise a one bedroom apartment, with all facilities, and are open to all men over 60 years of age, "*of good character and able bodied*". The architecture of these apartments comprises flint walls with stone quoins and dressings to the leaded window openings, with some spectacularly tall octagonal stone chimneys rising above, and silhouetted against, the warm tiled roofs.

To the east of the Master's Office and immediately juxtaposed to the Beaufort Tower, on the north face of the

The Brethen's Hall
*Once called the "Hundred Mennes Hall", built in the14th
century, as the central meeting and eating place, in a style which
could be described as "lavish architectural beauty". It was here
that "Brothers were wont to sit on gaudy-days, (i.e. feast days of
which there were five in the year), and awaken the listlessness of
age by memories of by-gone days." (Early 19ᵗʰ century guide-book)*

Inner Quadrangle, is the 14th Century **Brethren's Hall**.
The hall is approached by a short flight of stone steps, the
ground floor of the main building being raised above an
undercroft. Formerly the Master's Hall, the Brethren's Hall
was built in the 14ᵗʰ century. Inside, this great room has a

beautiful roof of Spanish chestnut arched trusses seen
above plain-plastered walls and a tiled floor. On the west
face is musicians' gallery with carved timber wainscot
panelling. Centrally placed, was the site of the original
fireplace, with no flue, the smoke escaping from an
aperture in the ceiling. The hall is lit by decorated Gothic
windows and in the glazing is featured the symbol of St.
Cross.

Leading from the Brethen's Hall is the **14ᵗʰ century
Kitchen** with its stone flagged floor and very high timber
ceiling lit by two large plain windows. Within this kitchen
some amazing implements are preserved, including an
enormous lead-lined sink over oak framing, and a most
elaborate kitchen range. This range consisted of roasting
spits, bread oven, a chamber for boiling water, and the spit
on which the meat was roasted which was driven by a large
fan in the chimney, this being driven in turn by the hot air
rising from the fire.

It is fortunate therefore that much of the Hospital of
St. Cross and its fine grounds are open to the public (except
Sundays). It is always intriguing to witness an
encapsulation of history in modern times, when ancient
buildings are still being used for their original purpose.
There is of course the fascination of thinking about the
logistics and funding of the great building work, which
make up this beautiful complex. The use of traditional
materials reflected not only local sources such as flint but
political influences also, in bringing stone from the quarries
in Caen, being the result of French administration and
thought. However, central to the whole matter of the
founding and building of The Hospital of St. Cross was
the power, influence and wealth of the church in the Middle
Ages, without whose patronage there would be but a
beautiful water meadow here today.

Riverside Gardens

This view of the River Itchen, near to the City Bridge, with the City mill behind and the riverside walk alongside, is one of the beauty spots of Winchester. Historically, this is where the eastern boundary of the town walls of Roman Winchester lay after the river had been diverted to accommodate the street pattern of one of England's earliest "new towns".

Chapter 7

OPEN SPACES

The River Itchen, of all the open spaces, is Winchester's pride and joy, and its waters provide the backdrop to some of its most venerable locations. To the south of the city lie the water meadows of St. Cross and a footpath from there meanders alongside the river, until Wharf Mill built in 1885 comes into sight. In the distance there is the view of the City Bridge and City Mill; while on the west bank are the great walls of Wolvesey Palace and beyond this views of Winchester College and the Cathedral.

Riverside Gardens is within the centre of this visual interest and the river there is only part of an interlacing system of streams and watercourses, some visible and others roaring underground and invisible within culverts. The main stream of the river here is quick-flowing with flecks of light playing upon the waters, while below the surface the gravel bed shines through a covering of multi-green water weeds. The sounds of wildlife pervade the air, while near to the City Bridge, in contrast, are seen mute swans and their cygnets who come here to feed on the profusion of water plants. Alongside the banks and to the east, house gardens tumble downwards to the riverside, where alongside a single footbridge there are two fine trees, one a copper beech and the other an ash to complete the scene of tranquillity. Near to the City Bridge are some walled gardens, with doors opening directly on to the river itself, with mellow brickwork playing host to a multitude of plants within the open joints of its walls. Just opposite on the other bank to the west, is the plaque marking the

remains of the old Roman Wall of the city to remind us again of the antiquity of this place.

The **River Itchen** is an example of a groundwater fed river, with its overall catchment area of some 400 square kilometres, where the rainfall soaks into the chalk substrata and there forms a massive underground reservoir or "aquifer". Today water for the public water supply is extracted from the river and from boreholes nearby at Otterbourne and Gater's Mill. From the 12th century onwards, the main stream of this river was navigable from Southampton Water to as far north as Alresford by barges and it was along this same route that stone for the Cathedral came as well as merchandise for trade. In the 17th century the "Itchen Navigation" canal was built with 17 locks through which waterborne traffic passed from Southampton to Winchester until it closed in 1869. In other words this river had been both a source of water supply and means of water transport over the centuries before the coming of the railway in Victorian times and the building of subsequent road networks.

At the **City Mill**, the water surging beneath its rooms has been over the centuries a source of power for driving the water wheel; its oak spokes and elm paddles form part of a splendid machine, for processing wool and grain were the mainstays of the local economy in medieval times and beyond. James Cooke built the present mill in 1743, although there has been a mill on this site since the reign of King Richard I (reigned 1189-99) when it was known

The City Mill
The City Mill, (formerly known as the Eastgate Mill), for centuries provided power for cornmilling, papermaking, tanning, and fulling (wool processing). There has been a mill on this site since the 12ᵗʰ Century, although one James Cooke in 1743 built the present mill.

as the Eastgate Mill. Originally the mill had monastic connections but later was controlled by the Crown. In 1554 the mill was given to the city by Queen Mary (reigned 1553-58) following the aftermath of her marriage to King Philip of Spain, and at that time was renamed the City

Mill. Afterwards, in 1820 the mill was sold by the Corporation to one John Benham, and for over a century or more had a useful working life until economic circumstances brought about decline and redundancy. Today the mill has been restored and is in the stewardship of the National Trust, and although no longer a working mill it receives visitors and plays host to the Youth Hostel Association.

Behind the mill is a small sequestered garden between two channels of the river, one slow moving and the other fast flowing, on what can best be described as a narrow "tongue" of land tapering to a point at the far end. Rubble stone walls reach down to the waters of the river, with a profusion of wild flowers nestling down to the water's edge, including gipsywort with white flowers seen next to a bright orange display of touch-me-not.

Turning right while leaving the City Mill, and almost immediately to the left, the **Abbey Gardens** come into view, with ornate iron railings along the road frontage and a parallel watercourse immediately behind, leading the eye to **Abbey House**, the Mayor of Winchester's official residence. This building originates from about 1750 although it was altered in 1771. It has a red brick façade with a pediment and sash windows on the park side elevation while on the front side there is a splendid oriel window above the front door, surmounted by a crenellated roofline. In other words there is a change in style from the Classical appearance at the rear to that of the front which is distinctly Gothic.

The grounds around Abbey House hark back to the great antiquity of this place, being the site of the **Nunnaminster** founded by Queen Aelhswith (wife of King Alfred) in A.D. 903. Quite nearby, between Abbey House and the Guildhall, excavations are open to public view

Abbey Gardens
The classical Georgian red brick façade of Abbey House forms the backdrop to the splendid view of the gardens, where within the "fragrance garden" for the visually impaired such species as perowskia, lavender, santolia, balm rue and lily of the valley, can be enjoyed on seating, set within the flowerbeds, immediately adjacent to the house.

confirming that this monastic foundation *"was one of the foremost centres of art and learning in England"*. The original foundation was rebuilt after the Norman Conquest, (no surprises here), in about A.D. 1100 when it became known as **St. Mary's Abbey**. It is recorded that the Abbey had at one time an establishment of 102, including 26 nuns teaching the children of the nobility.

The complex of the Abbey included a new church with a tower and cloisters in all *"built on a grand scale"*. Around the church were grouped the lodgings for the Abbess, a school, hospital, and indeed all the infrastructure for self-sufficiency including fishponds upstream on the river nearby (i.e. the Itchen), as well as a mill, the precursor of the present City Mill and on or near the same location. The excavations referred to previously show a central portion of the nave of the church and indicate that the foundations overall stretched from the site of the present Guildhall to nearby the present Abbey House. An interesting feature to the rear of Abbey House is a small garden with seats, laid out with planting relying on smell to allow for the partially sighted or those without vision to enjoy the fragrance of this truly splendid garden.

Abbey House

A detail of the Gothic front, with its mellow red brickwork, stone string courses, elegant oriel window and front door feature, seen through flamboyant iron gates and railings.

In the alleyways beyond this garden there is a small garden called "**Water Close**" which is both quiet and idyllic with a clear pond now bedecked with water lilies, but which was once the source of the original monastic water supply leading to The Close. It is now part of a private garden but open to public view; seen through the low ornate wrought iron balustrade at the front, and set against the backdrop of the east end of the Cathedral rising majestically above.

Moving further along through The Close itself and into College Street, and almost opposite the Headmaster's House, **College Street Gardens** are seen, designed we are told by "*an art master at the College*", nearby. It is strictly rectangular in shape, occupying the site of some now demolished houses and its planting is seen against a beautiful brick wall. There is an Indian bean tree, two cherry trees and an evergreen magnolia with a very tall oak tree as the centrepiece. The space created by this garden in the overall street scene acts as a successful foil to the sombre cliff-like facades to the medieval College buildings across the road, and to the Headmaster's House, while adding a little light relief. The garden is said to be in the style of the 1920's but, be that as it may, it most certainly is an example of the late days of the so-called "plant collectors" reflecting the work of Dean Garnier carried out earlier in The Close.

Returning to The Close, and just south of the Cathedral and the Slype, is the **Dean Garnier Garden** designed by Sally Hocking and laid out quite formally, with gravelled walks and divided into two sections by a pergola. This garden is named after Thomas Garnier, Dean of Winchester (1840-72), who was also a distinguished

Water Close

This garden of water plants marks the source of the original water supply to the Close, seen through a wrought ironwork balustrade, with the east end of the Cathedral rising majestically in the background.

horticulturalist and collector of rare plants. The garden is seen near to the stone arcading of the Chapter House, being part of the **Benedictine Priory of St. Swithun**. This Priory, established in A.D. 964 by Bishop Ethelwold (A.D. 963-84), was arranged around cloisters to the south of the Cathedral nave. After the Dissolution of the Monasteries most of the buildings were lost, and only the Chapter House arcading remains today as a reminder of this once great monastic foundation.

Moving out of The Close and upwards towards St. Thomas Street, there is an idiosyncratic garden on the site of the graveyard of the former St. Thomas' Church. Today gravestones are set into the lawns of two houses around this unusual walled garden. The main features of this garden surround a wedding cake tree, with its foliage set in tiers; a table topped clipped yew, and a magnolia tree. The whole garden is now set against the backdrop of the mellow red and grey brick facades of the houses with their arched windows and white painted sashes, nestling beneath tiled roofs with dormers.

At the Great Hall of Winchester Castle there is a remarkable garden reached through the interior of the Hall itself, called **Queen Eleanor's Garden** and immediately adjacent to the Military Barracks set on higher ground. This is a garden of exquisite delicacy, laid out in fact in 1986, but with designs based on a royal garden of the Middle Ages. Garden designs of this era were influenced by *"elaborate symbolism of flowers and plants"* when for instance the rose, iris and columbine held a religious significance.

The garden derives its name from two queens both called Eleanor, namely Eleanor of Provence, wife of King Henry 111 (reigned 1216-72), and Eleanor of Castile, wife of King Edward 1 (reigned 1272-1307). This garden is

Graveyard
This unique garden is on the site of the graveyard of the Church of St. Thomas, now on the grounds of 21-22 St. Thomas Street. The established and lush planting nestles around the gravestones and forms a seemingly natural setting for the late Georgian houses which lay well back, and parallel to the road.

linear in form with a lean-to dovecote at one end and a fountain, all diminutive in scale. The floor of the garden has formal paving and grassed areas, and the planting is equally ordered. There are medicinal herbs such as periwinkle, sage, hyssop, heartsease, and iris. In addition there are herbs grown for their fragrances exampled by southern wood, juniper, and fennel, together with strawberries both ornamental and nice to eat! The planting in the garden was therefore both practical and pleasing to look at. There is an interesting perspective overall brought about by the shape, content and context of this little garden; seen between the ecclesiastical and Gothic forms of the medieval Hall, and the classical shapes of the Barracks' buildings nearby.

On the fringes of Winchester are two great open spaces namely St. Catherine's Hill lying to the south-east, and St. Giles' Hill on line with the west to east thoroughfare of the city namely the High Street and The Broadway, from where it rises majestically to view.

St. Catherine's Hill always seems to have a distant and remote aura with its history going back into antiquity, being the site of an Iron Age fort. In the 12th century there was a chapel dedicated to St. Catherine, whose emblem in art is a wheel, and today is seen in what has been described as *"a mysterious maze"*, cut into the turf, and lying on the site of the chapel. The view of this hill is now dominated by the monumental cutting in the chalk nearby, with the M3 extension snaking by, which new road has provoked such controversy.

St. Giles' Hill, and the summit of its slopes was home in medieval times to the world-famous **St. Giles' Fair.** The granting of the right to hold this fair was assigned to the Church and Bishop Walkelin in the late 11th century to last for three days before, on and after the Feast of St. Giles,

Queen Eleanor's Garden
This is a garden of considerable historic interest and is based on a Royal Garden of the Middle Ages. The design is based on an "elaborate symbolism of flowers and plants", and derives its name from two Queens, namely Eleanor of Provence, wife of King Henry 111, and Eleanor of Castile, wife of King Edward 1.

the patron saint of cripples and the poor. The right to hold this fair was a considerable financial advantage both to the Church and the town, because at that time it was forbidden to carry out trade for its duration within "seven leagues" of Winchester. Consequently it became an unsurpassed success, drawing traders from far and wide, and at its height the duration of the fair was extended to some 16 days, at which time shops and roads had been built to support the enterprise.

Today St. Giles' Hill provides a brilliant vantagepoint

A view from St. Giles' Hill
St. Giles' Hill was the home of the medieval St. Giles' Fair,
granted by King Rufus to Bishop William Walkelin in the late
11ᵗʰ Century, and which was to become one of the greatest
trading fairs known throughout Europe.

to view the city, which inspired the artists who drew "The East Prospect of the City of Winchester in 1736". Again the eye is virtually level with the crenellated parapet of the Cathedral tower, although at that date there were no visitors on guided tours to punctuate the skyline of the tower silhouette. However the broad layout is the same, with Winchester College to the left, the Cathedral centre stage as it were, the line of the ancient High Street immediately to its right and the West Gate in the far background. However Wren's King's Palace is no longer there nor are other buildings which have not stood the test of time. New images have however, come in their place, most notable of all the interventions of the 20ᵗʰ century, commencing with the awesome statue of King Alfred the Saxon Warrior sited almost outside Winchester's Victorian Guildhall. The original street patterns are mainly there although modern roads and new developments have in some places blurred the image. However the planned forms of the Romans, Saxon and medieval street patterns still survive to give identity and visual cohesion to today's city.

Church of St. Lawrence-in-the-Square
St. Lawrence is the only surviving Norman church within the old city walls that serves as a parish church. (From a painting by the artist Wilfred Ball, published in 1909 in Telford Varley's book 'Hampshire'.)

Chapter 8

THE CITY CHURCHES
PAST AND PRESENT

Ecclesiastical influences are never far away in Winchester commencing with the domination of the medieval Cathedral, the longest in Europe of its class. Around this great church are gathered the Parish Churches of Winchester, which in the 19th century amounted to twelve in all, namely All Saints, St. Paul, Christ Church, St. Lawrence, St. Maurice, St. Swithun, St. Thomas and St. Clement, St. Michael, St. John the Baptist, St. Peter Chesil, St Bartholomew, and finally Holy Trinity then referred to as the "District Church". Of this number six were built in the Victorian era, St. Maurice in 1842, (incorporating a medieval tower), St. Thomas and St. Clement in 1845-6, Holy Trinity in 1853-4, Christ Church in 1861, St. Paul started in 1872, and finally All Saints built between 1890-8. The remainder are essentially medieval churches, although restored, apart from St. John the Baptist which retains much of its original 12th and 13th century fabric and 15th century furnishings and embellishments.

The mid 19th century has been chosen as a starting point because at that time there was a proliferation of new church building and reordering and restoration of medieval places of worship. This period in England's history saw a rapid rise in the population overall in the wake of the Industrial Revolution, and in addition to churches, schools and libraries were also built. The Victorians therefore had a seemingly evangelical zeal to cater for both the souls and minds of its people. It was at

The Church of St. Swithun-upon-Kingsgate
This church is unique in that it is the only remaining church above a Winchester City Gate. In Anthony Trollope's novel 'The Warden' published in 1855 the building is immortalised in the final chapter, as "This singular little Gothic building, perched over a gateway through which the Close is entered... It is no bigger than an ordinary room but still a perfect church."

this time also that both colour and decoration became in vogue for its buildings both ecclesiastical and municipal, all linked to the Arts and Craft Movement of the 19th century. Nowhere was this more evident than in its churches when the Gothic style was reintroduced and updated.

The **Church of St. Swithun-upon-Kingsgate** is unique in that it is the only church above a Winchester City Gate, although formerly there had been churches above both the North and East Gates, before they were demolished. The gateway itself comprises a main central arch, formerly for vehicles to pass through, with two later smaller arches either side for foot traffic. The present stone-built structure of the church above forms part of the original City Walls, and the arch beneath this originally provided access in and out of the city for the Priory of St. Swithun alongside the Cathedral. However, it is recorded that a feud arose between the citizens of Winchester and the monks of St. Swithun in the year 1264 when both the gatehouse and the church were severely damaged by fire. Following this the church and gatehouse were repaired. The present gateway is of the 14th century and the church above in its design is attributed to the 16th century. The side gateways are an 18th century addition. In other words, although there has been a church on this site since the 13th century, it has been subject to the vicissitudes of history, weather erosion and fashion, although maintaining its essentially medieval form through to the present day.

The church and gatehouse, viewed from the south side in College Street, combine the features of a fortification, i.e. the crenellated parapet with the solidity of the mainly flint walls. Just two windows to the church pierce these walls, both with a central stone mullion in a 16th century Gothic style. There are two substantial stone buttresses on either side of the central pointed arch, to complete the picture of solidity and strength. A domestic feeling emerges however with a glimpse of the red tiled pitched roof to the church and two dormer windows, which are seen behind the parapet.

The entrance to the church is via a long flight of timber stairs, approached from St. Swithun Street, inside a lean-to structure with a tiled roof and tile hung walls, alongside the house adjoining. The "nave" of the church at the top of these stairs comprises a small room of almost domestic proportions. There are two small windows facing south, and similarly two at the north side, the nearest to the east being the only one here with stained glass. At the east end, above the altar, there is a very simple stained glass window in muted tones of blue, yellow and green, containing glass taken from the Church of St. Peter Chesil, now redundant. On the west wall is a further stained glass window, and although there are two dormer windows high on the south, the church is quite dimly lit and mystical. Above this the roof of oak members of cross beams and angled supports form a pattern seen in contrast with the simple lime-washed plaster walls. Near the north-west door is a stone font, and at the head of the stairs is a plaque recording that, "*The English Oak Pews installed in 1968 mark the completion of the restoration of St. Swithun's Church.*" Over this plaque the beautiful oak half-timber and panels of brick noggins surround the staircase adding to the aura and antiquity of this truly solemn and holy place, at St. Swithun-upon-Kingsgate.

Moving northwards from St. Swithun's and through the St. Swithun Gate of The Close, and via the majestic avenue of lime trees over Cathedral Green, at the far end of Great Minster Street, the tower of the **Church of**

St. Lawrence-in-the-Square comes into view. There is a beautiful painting of this scene by the artist Wilfrid Ball, published in 1909 in Telford Varley's book "Hampshire". The square tower of the church is depicted rising above the surrounding buildings of red brick and tiled roofs, and the remarkable thing is that little has changed in essence to the present day.

The history of Winchester's past is embodied within this building, most significantly during the Commonwealth era of Cromwell, (1649-60), when beforehand in 1645 and following the siege of the city, churches were either destroyed or closed down. Of the Church of St. Lawrence in particular it is recorded that in 1660 "*...it was made a school, wherein are taught the children of the city*", while prior to the Civil War the church, "*was in the best repair of any in the city*". It was during this period, i.e. the Commonwealth, that the interior of St. Lawrence was cleared out, and the ecclesiastical furnishings removed, and it was not until 1672 that it reverted to a church. In modern times the ravages of time have taken their toll when in 1978, a fire caused much damage to the interior, and in line with its previous history, but for different reasons, the inside of the church was again restored. An entrance door beneath the tower on the west end leads via a vestibule into the main body of the church, the tower in plan being at a skew to the nave and again like its sister church, St. Swithun's, is just one room although this time of higher proportions. At high level there are double king post roof trusses in oak, with the east window beneath, which is an enlarged version of a former opening now blocked up at a lower level. The organ case and cantilevered carved timber screen and figureheads adorn the west end of the church. The vestry, which once occupied a space in the

Church of St. Maurice
Erected in 1842, although all that now remains of this fine church after fire struck is the former medieval tower, which now abuts Debenhams Department Store. Today this tower now serves as its fire escape from the top floor Cathedral View Restaurant, inside of which, the original stone and flint walls of its walls are left exposed.

tower, is now in a basement on the other side of the medieval vaulted undercroft, beneath Gilbert's Bookshop next door. (There is a staircase down to this basement within the shop, and at the end of the stone vaults is a wall where the division with the church vestry occurs.) On the 1873 Ordnance Map there is a delineation of the boundary of the extent of the Royal Palace of King William 1, shown hard against the east wall of the church and beyond. In the church guide it states, "*St. Lawrence is the only surviving Norman church within the old city walls that survives as a parish church*," and continues to suggest the "tradition" that the present church had its origins as the chapel of William the Conqueror's Palace. Be that as it may, there is a strong probability that the single cell plan shape may have had its beginnings in the 11th century. There is uncertainty as to whether the church at one time had a chancel, but it is recorded that the east window was "reconstructed" in 1449, which means that a chancel was not present at that time in its history. The Norman antecedents have tangible evidence in the form of a blocked-up 13th century doorway on the north wall, giving access at one time to the High Street. The church in its present form is authenticated by Bernard Woodward in his History of Winchester published in about 1860. A quoted document refers to "*…the founders and builders of this churche called Sainte Lawrence within the cittie of Winchester…in the year of our Lord God, 1449*". At that time there was a complete reconstruction including the east window to which reference has already been made above. This all coincides with the 15th Century dating given by Pevsner/Lloyd in the Hampshire volume of the Buildings of England series. Additional items of history given by Woodward record repairs to the tower roof in the year 1680, and in 1765 the construction of a side

gallery by the then Rector, the Rev. Mr Cotton, "*for the use of his scholars*", which has since been removed in the early 19th century.

Historically, the tower of the church and its bells have played an important role in the life of the city proclaiming both sad and joyful occasions. Originally there were five bells to be rung and in the St. Lawrence Church Register for 1715 there is an entry, "*For Ringers when the Rebbells was beate at Preston, 3s.*" This would presumably refer to an incident in the first Jacobite Rebellion. Today only one bell remains, namely the oldest dating from 1621, and a single bell had been used both to signal the time of curfew and at public executions in The Square nearby. On a happier note this same bell is still used at the enthronement of Bishops of Winchester, who first come to St. Lawrence Church in preparation, and having been presented to the Mayor of Winchester and citizens, then process to the Cathedral, led by the Churchwardens, for the ceremony

Just a short distance away is the **Church of St. Maurice**, likewise alongside the High Street, erected in 1842 and at that time consisting of both nave and chancel, two side aisles and vestry. However, today all that remains of this fine church is the former medieval tower, which like St. Lawrence Church, also had five bells. The tower had a chequered history, in that it was also the tower to a previous church which had burnt down. The Victorian Church of St. Maurice was demolished in 1957, leaving just the tower standing. Today this tower abuts the Debenhams Department Store, which was built in part over the site of the church, and where today there is a physical link between both store and tower, which now serves as a fire escape route! Within the Cathedral View Restaurant, on the second floor of Debenhams, the tower

Church of St. John
Overall this church is truly unspoilt and of remarkable integrity, and its great antiquity is further emphasised by the very site in which it stands above a 4th century Roman cemetery. From the outside the main body of the church is almost domestic in scale, with its flint walls nestling beneath red tiled roofs, entered on the south side by a brick and flint porch.

has been left exposed with its original stone and flint walls, which comes as no small surprise and great excitement, being a spectacular example of finding a new use for a redundant historic structure. The inside of the tower can also be viewed from this level with its low-pitched pyramidal roof and covering of slates and disused steel bell-frames below.

At the base of the tower is a fine Norman doorway, with typical dog-tooth embellishments within its semicircular stone arch. Above this at an intermediate level are twin lancet windows framed in brickwork and again at belfry level are similar lancet windows but of a larger scale. The walls of the tower are built in an equal measure of stone and flint in a chequered pattern, while at the corners the quoins are formed in dressed stone. There are substantial stone buttresses at the south-west and south-east corners, the former at 45 degrees and the latter at right angles to the main wall. The Norman doorway and open space alongside provide a pedestrian access from the High Street to St. Maurice's Covert, and part of the paving is made up of grave headstones laid flat. One such stone bears the inscription *"Here lyeth the body of Benjamin Clarke Esq. Who dyed October 5th 1618 in the third time of his mayoralty aged 71."* Other burials now unmarked are recorded in the Parish Registers and in the period between 1643-6 there are several entries for the burial of soldiers killed in the civil wars of the Commonwealth era. In other words there has been a church on the site since late Elizabethan time at least although the Norman work on the tower would suggest antecedents back to the 11-12th century.

On the other side of the River Itchen to the east and across the City Bridge, are two churches, namely the **Church of St. John**, in St. John Street, and close by, the

Church of St. Peter Chesil, in Chesil Street. Both churches are medieval, but only the Church of St. John has stood the test of time and remains a place of worship, the fabric of which is best preserved in respect of its original architectural features. St. Peters' Chesil is now a redundant church, but has entered into a new life as the home of the Winchester Dramatic Society, although still retaining the aura of a church notwithstanding an almost foreboding appearance because of its grime encrusted façade. Three roads radiate from the east end of Bridge Street, namely St. John Street reached off Magdalen Hill and finally Chesil Street running almost parallel to the River Itchen in a north-south direction. From the lower end of St. John Street the road rises gently with a narrow space between terraced red brick houses. Towards the top on the left-hand side the view opens up to reveal St. John's Church and its quaint little churchyard perched advantageously with a view across the city.

From the outside the main body of the church is almost domestic in scale, with its flint walls nestling beneath red tiled roofs, and entered on the south side by a brick and flint porch. There is a crennelated parapet to the Gothic tower alongside the porch at the south-west corner of the church. Inside there is a church of rare beauty, almost square in plan made up of three aisles or arcades, comprising a central nave and chancel, with side aisles, each part of which originally had an altar at the east end. The arcades of the nave have circular stone columns with almost semicircular arches. On closer inspection the arches above the columns are slightly pointed at the apex, in other words in a transitional Norman to Early English Gothic style dating from about 1142. According to the church guide this dating makes it one of Winchester's oldest churches. The nave and

The Church of St. Peter Chesil
This church is 12th century in origin, formerly called "St. Peter Cheesehill". The 13th century tower is built in four stages with a pyramidal roof. Inside the tower, through its various stages, are some massive oak frame members, acting as bracing for the external walls, while at bell-chamber level there is outside a cladding of plain tile hanging. The grime and smoke encrusted stone quoins together with their flint walls somehow enrich the integrity of this medieval church.

chancel are divided by a 14th century rood screen of carved timber, in front of which is a 15th century timber pulpit. Originally the three altars at the east end were visually interconnected for the priests by "squints" (medieval vision panels), and the three spaces further divided by very intricate 14th century "parclose" screens separating the chancel and sanctuary from the side chapels. Today the church organ dating from 1877 has replaced the altar previously in the north aisle. The windows within the church are of special interest, for instance the 13th century windows on the south wall of the Lady Chapel; while on the west wall of the north aisle is part of a blocked Norman window. Of special note also are the wall paintings on the north wall inside niches dating from 1280 and discovered when the lancet windows, in which the niches are placed came to light in 1958. The baptistery placed at the east end contains a 15th century font nearby to which in the nave aisle is a large and splendid brass candelabrum, suspended from the ceiling, retaining still its wax candles. Overall this church is truly unspoilt and of remarkable integrity, and its great antiquity is further emphasised by the very site on which it stands above a 4th century Roman cemetery.

The Church of St. Peter Chesil is 12th century in origin, formerly called "St. Peter upon Chesulle without (i.e. outside Eastgate). The building stands on a tight site between Chesil Street and the River Itchen, and has a very compact plan, with a square tower at its south-east corner, immediately adjacent to the south aisle with the nave on its north side. Both nave and aisle are seen gable-end on to the road and face east with the nave roof rising to a higher level than the narrower south aisle. The main view therefore of the church is from the road, while from the west the tower can be seen rising above the trees in the gardens running down to the river bank. The tower is built in four stages, with its pyramidal tiled roof surmounted by a modern weathervane dated 1984, to mark the building's restoration by the Winchester Preservation Trust.

Inside the tower, through its various stages, are some massive oak frame members, acting as bracing for the external walls of flint and stone in chequered pattern, while at bell-chamber level there is outside a cladding or plain tile hanging. The interior of the church, now redundant, has been converted to use as an intimate theatre, and is home to the Winchester Chesil Theatre. All the original church fittings are now removed, and are either lost or in a new home. For instance the late Norman font of Petworth Marble is now seen at All Saints Church in Petersfield Road, and some stained glass has been relocated in St. Swithun's Church, as previously stated. Originally there were galleries inside the nave, one of which gave access to the house next door, and the outline of the doorway can still be seen high on the north wall. Of this feature a then contemporary writer observed, "*the persons from the adjoining house can participate in the service without leaving their home*".

The nave and aisle are subdivided by an arcade of three arches with circular stone columns and arches in the transitional Norman style, the spaces between the columns having since been part walled up to increase the stability of the building. The church nave retains two windows in the transitional Decorated style on the east wall and one similar window on the west side. The original main entrance to the church is from a door on the north elevation, next to which is a square-headed window of a later date and style than the others.

The Parish Registers give some insight into the role

Holy Trinity Church
This is an impressive Victorian church constructed during the period 1853-4 at a cost of £4500. By way of a final touch of grandeur there is a fine approach to the west doors, via an avenue of lime trees, which frame the carved stone porch, almost Art Nouveau in its design.

of this small church in the Middle Ages. For instance at the time of the plague in 1665-6, some of its worst effects were noted along with measures taken to cope with the devastating effect of this catastrophe. The Parish of Chesil was particularly affected, and some entries of deaths in the Register were marked with the letter "O" to denote the spots of the fatal malady (i.e. smallpox). Isolation for those stricken with the disease was enforced by the maintenance of a "thatched pest house", while others were literally incarcerated in their homes. For instance there is an entry for "*an eyron strap to fasten the Sherod's door, 3d*". Notwithstanding the seemingly harsh measures adopted to combat the spread of infection, there was much compassion, albeit combined with fear, for those afflicted. This is confirmed by evidence of "*notices of relief*", i.e. help, for the victims of the "visitation" and marked down in these same records. It is a remarkable fact that in the Parish of St. John nearby there was at that time almost no evidence of the disease. This phenomenon was commented upon by Samuel Pepys, who on visiting a nearby Hampshire town wrote, "*one side of the street had almost every house infected through the town, and the other not one shut up*".

Holy Trinity Church stands within a grassed and walled site, parallel and adjacent to the North Walls and between Upper Brook and Middle Brook Streets. This is an impressive Victorian church, with flint walls, stone dressings to its windows, and embraced by robust buttresses, while above is a very steeply sloping slate roof surmounted by a delicate fleche feature, defining the division between the nave and sanctuary inside. The carved stone porch at the west end is almost Art Nouveau in design, and is in contrast with the near severity of the main exterior. The architect, Henry Woodyer, produced

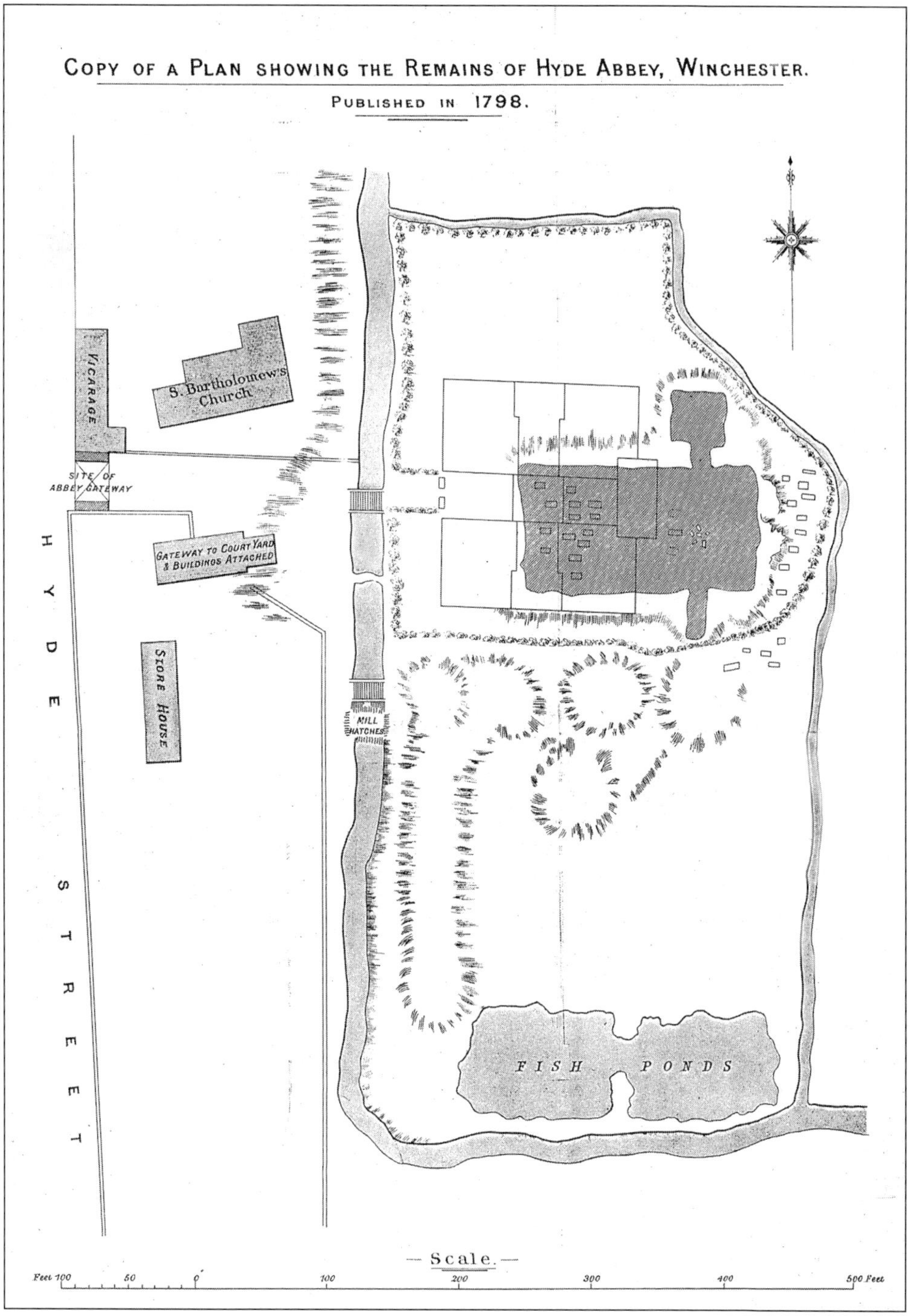

COPY OF A PLAN SHOWING THE REMAINS OF HYDE ABBEY, WINCHESTER.

PUBLISHED IN 1798.

VICARAGE

S. Bartholomew's Church

SITE OF ABBEY GATEWAY

GATEWAY TO COURTYARD & BUILDINGS ATTACHED

STORE HOUSE

MILL HATCHES

HYDE STREET

FISH PONDS

Scale.

Feet 100   50   0   100   200   300   400   500 Feet

**The Parish Church of
St. Bartholomew, Hyde**
*The siting of this church
figures in a map of 1798, (held
by the Hampshire Record
Office), entitled "Remains of
Hyde Abbey".*

The Parish Church of St. Bartholomew, Hyde
Situated outside the North Walls of the city, originally built for the servants of Hyde Abbey nearby. In 1857-9 the church was partly rebuilt by the architect John Colson. Parts of the structure are Norman in origin, for example the south porch doorway dating from circa 1130.

a design in Victorian Gothic style, and according to the informative Church Guide, it was constructed during the period 1853-4. However according to Bernard Woodward in his 1860 History of Winchester, wrote *"it was commenced in February 1852, and consecrated in July 1854"*. From the same source it is recorded that the land cost £900 and the building £4500.0.

The interior is in stark contrast to the plain exterior, with its lofty and dramatic proportions of the seven- bay nave and chancel. There is no real subdivision of these two spaces, while above is an exciting arch-braced timber roof structure side lit by clerestorey windows. The steeply sloping roof surfaces are brightly painted with a profusion of motifs, and below, the plain aisle walls, (which once contained wall paintings of The Stations of the Cross), are nevertheless adorned with beautiful stained glass windows by Messrs. Clayton and Bell. These windows installed in the late 1880's depict scenes from the Old Testament in the north aisle and the New Testament in the south aisle, including a poignant depiction of the Parable of the Good Samaritan. The wall paintings referred to above were carried out by Joseph A. Pippet before 1889, but have sadly been overpainted because the images had deteriorated to such an extent, although a detailed photographic record was made beforehand.

Following the construction of the church, the pulpit, chancel screen, and parclose choir screens were added after 1880, and all this timber-work is flamboyantly carved, together with the delicate choir stalls, with carving picked out in gold and blue. All this intricate detail, viewed together with the chequered marble floor in the Sanctuary, adds to the richness of the interior, over and above the colours in the ceiling and stained glass throughout. In every respect this is a typically Victorian

Church of St. Bartholomew, Hyde
View of the Norman work in the in the south porch.

church visually exciting both externally, and by contrast internally, taken with its richness of colour and detail almost to sentimental extremes. By way of a final touch of grandeur there is a fine approach to the west doors via an avenue of lime trees, leading thereafter to the interior where not all the "sittings", i.e. pews were free. An example of the social divisions of the era which extended throughout society and into its religion.

The **Parish Church of St. Bartholomew Hyde** is situated outside the North Walls of the city, originally built for the servants of Hyde Abbey nearby. Although the church was partly rebuilt in 1857-9, by the architect John Colson, and again in 1979-80 when alterations to the north side of the church took place, parts of the structure are Norman in origin, for example the south porch doorway dating from circa 1130. There is however a plaque on the south wall inside stating *"Church Restored 1856-62"*, suggesting that there was a wider programme of repairs being effected at about the same time as Colson was at work on the chancel.

The siting of the church figures in a map of 1798, (held in the Hampshire Record Office), entitled *"Remains of Hyde Abbey Winchester"*. The church is shown adjacent to and inside the "site of the Abbey Gateway" and north of the "Gateway to the Courtyard", which structure still exists. It is on this latter gateway that there is a plaque which reads *"Site of Hyde Abbey 1110. Burial place of Alfred the Great, his Queen and their Son Edward the Elder"*. (Hyde Abbey was the Benedictine nunnery founded in A.D. 965 as the New Minster and then sited to the north of the present Cathedral, before moving to the present site in A.D. 1110.)

St. Bartholomew's Church has a square west tower with a pyramidal roof; the walls are flint faced, with

Church of St. Paul

This Church was built in stages because of shortage of funds, while the tower and spire, being part of the original plans, by the architects Colson Senior and Junior, were never completed. Nevertheless, this is a lovely Victorian church, with the chancel having been consecrated in 1872.

diagonal stone buttresses at the south-west and north-west corners. Apart from the Norman work in the south porch, there are some single light windows on the south wall, and of what can be called "architectural fragments" taken from Hyde Abbey. Inside the south porch is *the ancient Stoup, i.e. vessel to contain holy water, of the Church of Hyde Abbey*", found in 1879, (again in the abbey grounds), and placed there by the Church Wardens.

Standing inside the church, the varying messages of history and time, relating to the various phases of this building, are difficult to comprehend. However having accepted that a church has stood on this site since Norman times, and that the structure has been altered and extended over the centuries, the pieces of the architectural jig-saw fall into place. The internal ambience of this church is quiet and serene. There is a beautifully carved chancel screen, inscribed with the words *"By thy Cross and Passion Good Lord Deliver Us"*, in the typically Victorian tradition. Within the chancel there are choir stalls and an organ case on the south side, and in the Lady Chapel a permanent light shines to denote the presence of the Holy Sacrament. Overall this is a little gem of a church set amid a small and tranquil churchyard, but not far distant from both the ancient Hyde Abbey site and the hustle and bustle of modern Winchester.

To the west of Winchester and its railway station, on high ground and overlooking the city, is the **Church of St. Paul**. Around about there is a quintessentially suburban setting leading towards the village of Weeke where the "mother church" of St. Matthew stands on the Stockbridge Road. St. Paul's church was built in stages, and because of shortage of funds the tower and spire of the original design were never built. The architects for

Church of St. Paul
Inside the church, above the Choir stalls is a small fragment of a mural depicting the parable of The Good Samaritan, by the artist Heywood Sumner.

the building were John Colson senior who died in 1894 leaving his son to complete the project. The Chancel was consecrated in 1872 on the 27th of July by the Bishop of Winchester, and the nave and transepts added in 1889, while the north and south aisles came in 1902 and 1910 respectively, the work of Colson junior.

Internally the church has an unusual plan in that the south aisle is wider than the north aisle, although the

Christ Church
This church carried out to completion in 1861 to the designs of the architect Ewan Christian, complete with its soaring broach spire; its foundation stone having been laid on the 28th September 1859.

logic of this can be explained in that both aisles are of different dates and the southern aisle was extended in width to accommodate the Lady Chapel. The nave of the church is of five bays in the Early English Gothic style, of splendid proportions with a soaring roof-space of timber-arched braces, resting on carved stone corbels in the walls. In the chancel there is by contrast a barrel timber roof and the east window below is a fine example of stained glass. Above the choir stalls on the south side on the plain painted walls, there is an exciting but small area of mural, recently restored as a trial project, which gives an insight into the images now painted over.

The subject of the mural fragment seen is that of The Good Samaritan, and was painted by the artist Heywood Sumner in a technique called "sgraffito". This is a decorative technique in which tinted plaster is covered with a thin layer of white plaster, the top layer then being scratched with a design revealing the lower layer. Heywood Sumner was a friend of William Morris, and influenced therefore by the ideals of the Arts and Crafts Movement of the late 19th century. George Heywood Maunoir Sumner, to give him his full name, was born in 1853; his father, George Sumner was Rector of Alresford and later Bishop of Guildford, and his grandfather, Charles Sumner, was sometime Bishop of Winchester. In other words Sumner had excellent ecclesiastical connections, and carried out artistic work of significance in several churches including his "masterpiece" at St. Agatha's Church in Portsmouth in 1901, (i.e. the decoration of the dome and apse in sgraffito).

Externally the church is constructed overall in grey stone of a somewhat sombre aura, with the three gables of the nave and aisles expressed at the west face, and entrance effected by a simple porch on the south-west

Christ Church
Mural detail now hidden from view and awaiting restoration behind screens, within the apse at the east-end.

corner. Although neither the tower nor spire was built, the lofty siting of this church overseeing the whole of Winchester is adequate compensation.

The building of **Christ Church** in Christ Church Road was carried out to completion in 1861 to the designs of Ewan Christian, and sited on high ground to the north of Southgate Street and to the west of the Peninsula Barracks. This church is complete with a broach spire and marks a departure from the norm in that the walls are built in stone throughout rather than the grey knapped flints used elsewhere in some city churches. The foundation stone seen in the apsidal end of the nave is dated 28th September 1859, and records the founder Charles Simeon who was born 100 years earlier.

Since the building of this church significant changes have come about with a modern "reordering", with the altar now at the west end together with a mosaic lined baptistery, and the original sanctuary now laid out as a meeting place. However, the original architectural features of the three-bay nave remain, with pointed stone arches and flamboyant capitals with a motif of grapes above circular red marble shafts and ponderous stone bases. The walls are plain and in the apse large timber folding doors provide a discreet screen to murals requiring restoration, encapsulated in this way for protection. The whole interior is very light and new seating and furnishings give the building a new image and modern appearance. Alongside the north aisle there is a modern glazed link to the Parish Office and other ancillary parts of the building, alive with the comings and goings of people other than on a Sunday. This is a remarkably friendly and welcoming church coming to terms with the 20th century and beyond.

The **Church of St. Thomas and St. Clement** stands

The Congregational Church (now United Reformed) of 1853 in Jewry Street.
A yellow bricked building in the Early English gothic style by the architect W.F. Poulton.

The Church of St. Thomas and St. Clement
Standing in Southgate Street, is by the far the most monumental of Winchester's Victorian churches. Built in 1845-6 and designed by the architect E.W. Elmslie, while the steeple was added in 1857. A plaque placed at the roadside records the fact that "reference to St. Thomas Church is made by Thomas Hardy, 1840-1928, in his novel 'Tess of the D'Urbervilles', first published in 1891" . (The precise reference was to the steeple, for which commission the original architect had to compete with other designers!)

in Southgate Street, and is by far the largest and most monumental of Winchester's Victorian churches. It was built in 1845-6 and designed by E.W. Elmslie, and was an enlarged replacement of the church in St. Thomas Street now demolished, with only the graveyard remaining as a private garden. Although in the main this church is designed in the Decorated Gothic style, it is *"no longer uniformed in its Gothic motifs and their handling"*, (Buildings of England, Pevsner/Lloyd). Its adorning feature is without doubt its great spire, which serves as an unmistakable landmark feature on the west side of the city. St. Thomas and St. Clement is no longer a church, and now serves as a centre of various organisations relating to Hampshire County Council, and before this as the Hampshire Record Office, now transferred to an equally remarkable new building near to the North Walls. A plaque at the entrance to the church reads, *"reference to St. Thomas Church is made by Thomas Hardy, 1840-1928, in his novel Tess of the d'Urbervilles, first published in 1891"*.

Moving further south of the city, and outside the line of its walls, lies the **Church of St. Michael**, sited parallel to St. Michael's Road, being the church used by the "Commoners" of Winchester College, and referred to in "Notions" as "Michla". The building is medieval in origin, but enlarged and much restored by the architect William Butterfield, and according to a plaque on the south wall, *"repaired and enlarged A.D.1822, Reverend G. Cox, Rector"*.

The church is built with a combination of grey flint walls and stone dressings. There is a porch on the south side, and at the west end is a squat square tower with diagonal buttresses at each corner, and a pyramidal tiled roof above. On the south side are the remains of a small

Church of St. Michael
Sited parallel to St. Michael's Road, being the church used by the "Commoners" of Winchester College, and referred to in "Notions" as "Michla". The building is medieval in origin, but enlarged and much restored by the architect William Butterfield in 1822 according to a plaque on the south wall.

sundial, which has lost its dial, but is fascinating nevertheless. Inside, the original nave and Victorian chancel extension to the east are in marked contrast in style and detail. Over the main body of the nave there is a continuous low-pitched curved ceiling, incorporating a side aisle to the north, giving the space an oddly unbalanced feeling. There is a fine pulpit, in carved timber, in memory of Henry Edward Moberly Rector from 1883-1907. The chancel has by contrast a symmetrical barrel roof, separated from the nave by a Gothic lancet arch. Outside the church on its north side is an unexpected garden of great beauty and calmness, in the centre of which is a giant sequoia as its centrepiece.

All Saints Church, Petersfield Road, was built to the designs of J.L. Pearson in 1890-8, and not entirely finished, as the protracted building programme would suggest. The church is built in two equal aisles, the south aisle being the nave and chancel, while the north aisle incorporates the Lady Chapel at the west end and vestry to the east. Externally the walls are built in the local flint, with brick quoins, and the buttresses are in similar materials with natural stone weatherings. On the south side are the beginnings of a tower, which was started but never finished, almost as though the builders had abruptly left and not come back, for whatever reason. There is a story that the incumbent suffered a fatal seizure at the dedication ceremony, but details of this event are scant. However, the incomplete nature of the nevertheless attractive church is all part of its history, linked no doubt with finance and Parish affairs over a century ago.

Returning to the exterior the windows are in mellow stone plate tracery of the transitional Early English style. Internally the church is plain and unadorned with an arcade of pointed arches separating the nave from the

All Saints Church, Petersfield Road
This church was built to the designs of the architect J.L Pearson during the period 1890-8. On the south side are the beginnings of a tower, which was started but never finished, almost as though the builders had abruptly left and had not come back, in an absence now lasting over 100 years!

Lady Chapel. At the west end of the nave is a late Norman font taken from St. Peter's Chesil when the latter church became redundant. It has been suggested that All Saints Church, tucked away in the Bar End district of Winchester, was built to serve the railway community there in Victorian times. Originally there was a branch line from the main Southampton to Winchester line, serving Alresford to the east and Whitchurch to the north, the route of which can clearly be seen today, running parallel with and to the east of Chesil Street. There is evidence today of this railway in the form of the blocked up tunnel at the end of Old Station Approach, behind the present day Winchester City Council Offices in Chesil Street. The brick built cottages around and about the church, represent the past working nature of this part of the city when steam driven trains were seen here, harking back to an era now passed.

King Alfred's College
Engraving published in the London News 25 October 1862 of the
West Hill Diocesan Training College, opened 13 October 1862 by
the Bishop of Winchester, (now King Alfred's College).
The Architect John Colson designed this building, although now
much altered in its architectural detail. (Reproduced by courtesy
of the Diocese of Winchester.)

Chapter 9

WINCHESTER'S NOTABLE INSTITUTIONS

To the west of the city centre in Romsey Road are two unmistakable landmark buildings, namely the H.M. Prison Winchester to the north side, and the Royal Hampshire County Hospital almost opposite on the south side of the same road. These two buildings represent by their very size, significant contributions to the architectural scene. A high and ominous brick wall shields the prison because of its function, while the hospital by contrast presents its façade of beautifully patterned brick walls to the road, although the view today is marred by the plethora of car parks and ancillary buildings. Both buildings are of a similar age; the prison was built in 1848-50, designed by the architect Pearse, while the hospital came to fruition in 1864-8, to designs by the eminent Victorian architect William Butterfield. The expanding population of Victorian England gave cause to replace and enlarge the former gaol in Jewry Street dating from 1805, and the hospital in Colebrook Street established in 1736. Both buildings are forerunners of the buildings seen today and are linked by a strange correlation in that while wrongdoing led to imprisonment, sin was formerly thought to be the cause of illness and in religious terms a form of retribution. For instance, at the entrance to the Colebrook Street hospital a text above the gateway read *"Despise thou not the chastising of the Almighty"*.

In dealing with the history of Winchester the use of the word "hospital" in relationship with its buildings has two specific meanings. In one sense the word hospital refers specifically to the care of the sick and lame, in another sense it means a charitable institution for the poor and needy, where part of its remit was to provide medical care for its residents. Within the first category will fall the hospitals in Colebrook Street, Parchment Street, and latterly the Royal Hampshire County Hospital in Romsey Road. The second category will include the Hospital of St. John, Christ's Hospital, and the Hospital of St. Mary Magdalene. Other ancillary medical foundations were provided by such places as the "Dispensary" in two houses, namely 5-6 The Square, set up in 1875 as a charity to serve those without the ability to pay for medicines and treatment.

One Dr. Alured Clarke, (1695-1742), founded a medical hospital in Colebrook Street, which was *"opened for the reception of patients on St. Luke's Day, October 18th 1736"*. Dr. Clarke was also Canon and Prebendary of Winchester Cathedral and some time Royal Chaplain. The building he chose and leased was previously a run-down medieval building, which he arranged to be converted and restored as a small hospital for some sixty in-patients. Although the building was demolished in 1959, a record drawing exists made by the then Cathedral architect N.C.H. Nesbitt in about 1914, showing a two-storey "L" shaped building, with both men's and women's wards on the first floor and ancillary rooms and physician's quarters on the ground floor. This was the first hospital in Winchester, and said to be then the only establishment of its kind outside of London. A few years later, another

Hospital Museum and Archive
Details of William Butterfield's Chapel, now used in part as the Hospital Museum and Archive, showing the decorative ceilings.

hospital was opened in Parchment Street, with a capacity for 128 patients, but unlike Colebrook Street, was purpose built to designs prepared by John Wood of Bath, and this time funded by a legacy from Richard Taunton of Southampton.

In a Hampshire County Hospital's Report, published by the Hampshire Chronicle Office, the "Final Report" contains an illuminating insight into the foundation of the present **Royal Hampshire County Hospital** now sited on the south side of Romsey Road on the outskirts of the City of Winchester. This report is in effect a summation of the whole thought process of the Committee appointed by the Court of Governors, in January 1862, to put into effect the purchase of the land, and for erecting the new hospital. The Rev. Robert S. Barter, Warden of Winchester College, had first mooted the idea of a new hospital after the feasibility of enlarging and updating the existing hospital

in Colebrook Street was found to be impractical. In the spring of 1863, the new hospital site of *"about 5 1/2 acres"* was purchased, *"unrivalled in the salubrity of its situation"*. Of the new building on this site it was agreed that, "an architect of first rate eminence be commissioned", and the Building Committee thereafter appointed William Butterfield for the task. The records show that the Committee were well pleased with their choice of architect, wherein they say, *"The external beauty of the building, which has since its completion excited so much admiration, is due almost entirely to its form and colour"*. The plans for the building had been overseen by Florence Nightingale, and were therefore pronounced, *"to be such as would produce a model hospital"*. Documentary evidence would however suggest that there had been a seeming difficulty in reconciling the final costs of the building with the original budget. It was soon realised that an increase in the cubic

Hospital Museum and Archive
Details of William Butterfield's Chapel showing part of the east window by Clayton and Bell.

capacity of air space per patient, over previous military hospitals, from 1500 to 2000 cubic feet, on the recommendation of Miss Nightingale, was the reason for this increase. However in the final analysis the total cost of the hospital building was £24,713, 1s, 11p, which for the 108 bed spaces worked out at about £230.00 per bed, which compared favourably with such establishments elsewhere.

Much of the cost of the building was met by private subscriptions, and William Butterfield personally donated £500 towards the cost of the Chapel. Most significantly however Queen Victoria sanctioned an annual subscription of £100 and *"by the communication from the Secretary of State of her Majesty's commands that the Hospital should be styled Royal"*. Within the *"Statutes of the Institution"*, dated 21st October 1857 it was decreed that the hospital should be *"open for the relief of the sick or disabled poor persons"*.

The regulation of the hospital was controlled by a Board of Governors comprising all donors of £50 or more, subscribers of 2 guineas annually, Parish Clerics providing a donation of £100 or more, together with the Chaplain and all physicians and surgeons. The hospital was then open to all subscribers for 10s, 6p, for three out-patients, £1, 1s, for one in-patient and three out-patients or six out-patients and so on prorata! In other words it was the Victorian equivalent of the modern private patient's schemes, with one important difference that urgent and accident patients could be admitted without payment, *"at any hour of the day or night"*, on the recommendation of the House Surgeon or Matron.

William Butterfield's building was quite clearly an innovative design visually, notwithstanding its functional purpose. Horizontal in form and essentially arranged on three to four floors, as well as below-ground

Hospital of St. John
Almshouses completed in 1833 on the earlier south range, as carried out to the designs of the architect William Garbett, (facing Colebrook Street).

accommodation, its asymmetrical facades are punctuated by turrets and other projecting staircase features, while some Gothic inspired architectural features in the form of pointed arches and stone tracery adorn the walls and windows. Perhaps the most striking feature overall is the use of blue "diaper" patterning and other intricate ornamentation within the red brick walls, giving an overall effect of richness achieved by very simple means. In addition the varied geometry of the roof elements, like the turrets, bay windows and gables, gives the building an exciting sculptural silhouette to its skyline.

Although none of the original plans exist, (Butterfield is thought to have destroyed them), an Ordnance Plan of 1873 gives a good indication of the layout of the ground floor and disposition of the vertical circulation. The main building is arranged east to west across the site, with the north elevation facing Romsey Road and the south elevation overlooking the Hospital Gardens. The hospital plan is divided into three main elements, with a central staircase and wards on either side. There were five large wards in all, two on the ground floor for men, two at first floor for women, while on the second floor level the hospital Chapel faced to the east and the west wing contained the fifth large ward. The turrets previously referred to contained bathrooms and other sanitary facilities, and the central staircase and circulation block housed operating theatre facilities and accommodation for the medical staff, and patient balconies off the wards. All in all this building seemed to be the "model hospital" predicted at the outset of construction, but events in the years after the opening of the building in 1868 proved otherwise for William Butterfield. Problems were to arise with the water supply and sewerage system to the hospital arising from the fact that at the time of construction there

Hospital of St. John the Baptist
Detail of carved figurehead on entrance arch to the south range.

resigned as the consultant to the hospital. It is not uncommon, over a period of time for relationships to founder in this way, but history will confirm that William Butterfield left behind a building masterpiece of that flamboyant Victorian era, in which he worked with such distinction.

Moving back in time, and to the lower end of the High Street, near to King Alfred's great statue, there are two ranges of almshouses to be found on both sides of The Broadway. **The Hospital of St. John the Baptist** and **Lamb's Almshouses** here represent one of Winchester's oldest charitable institutions, founded in 1289 by John Devenishe, *"citizen and alderman of cittie of Winchester"*, for the relief of sick and lame soldiers, pilgrims and wayfaring men, *"to have their dyett and lodging"*, for one night or longer. In 1558 Ralph Lamb, bequeathed £400 for the purchase of additional land to be conveyed to the "Master and Brethren" of the original foundation. The Chapel on the north side of the High Street and the adjoining St. John's House today represent the oldest buildings. The latter building served the dual purpose of both hospital, with the kitchen and dining room within the great hall on the first floor. The Chapel fell into disuse after the Reformation then in 1710 became in turn a school, although in 1838 it was repaired and re-consecrated as a place of worship.

The architect William Garbett designed the almshouses in the southern complex, and rainwater heads with dates suggest a building programme over the years 1817-33. The buildings are arranged around a courtyard, with a gatehouse facing the High Street, a moulded stone arch to the surrounding brick walls, and fine carved heads at the springing of the arch. The accommodation is arranged primarily on two storeys, with two tones of brick,

was no mains drainage available for the chosen site. The architect had been obliged to design a private system of drainage dispersal arrangements, which over a period of time gave cause for concern. In spite of Butterfield's best endeavours to address the problems, which seemed to arise from inadequate maintenance, friction arose between the architect and management. In a letter dated 22nd May 1880, 12 years after the opening of the hospital, Butterfield

defining the window openings and gable features by contrast. On the Colebrook Street façade at roof level there are clusters of joined octagonal chimney stacks nestling elegantly above the sloping clay tiles.

Immediately opposite the almshouses to the north of the southern complex, other almshouses are set back behind the Chapel, at right angles to the High Street, and running from south to north. The houses here are of a different character and more ornate, with fine red brick walls, stone quoins and surrounds to both door and window openings, with pretty brick porches having patterned slate roofs, as well as at main roof level. In addition there are clustered chimney stacks again which register greatly on the eye because the wide lawns and paths in front allow scope to stand back and enjoy the view. These houses look less austere than the sequestered courtyards of the south range, but this is a subjective observation rather than fact.

Central to the whole complex of the Hospital of St. John is the **Chapel** and adjoining **St. John House**, situated facing the road on the north side of the High Street. The Chapel was endowed in 1428, although the lancet windows in the flint walls suggest an earlier date. St. John's House is a remarkable looking building with 13th century lancet windows at ground level, while the upper floor is all rendered and is of the 18th century; its six great sash windows are distinctly Georgian as is the room inside. At a higher level there are "windows" which on closer inspection are but painted replicas! Internally the undercroft retains much of its medieval features with its stone flagged floors and rough masonry walls with indents that carried previous timber beams now removed. The first-floor room is a great surprise due to its size, and particularly its height and the florid wall decorations of garland

The north range of almshouses
Built in 1852, these later and more ornate dwellings than those on the south range, adjoin the historic nucleus of the establishment, namely St. John's Chapel and St. John's House.

motives. This room is no longer used by the hospital but historically is the location of its original dining hall and kitchens.

On the north side of Cathedral Green are some very attractive buildings, constructed in mellow red brick with white painted casement windows and double linked brick arches marking the entrances with their white painted doors. Above the two-storey facades are dormer windows set within the clay tiled roof; and the whole picture is seen framed by the iron railings, protecting the paths and gardens in front of the terrace of 10 dwellings. These properties are known as **Bishop Morley's College**, an institution founded in 1672 as the College of Matrons, and endowed for *"The widows of ten poor clergymen of this Diocese and that of Worcester"*. The present buildings however date from 1880 and were designed by the architects John Colson and John B. Colson, father and son, who also designed St. Paul's Church in Winchester. Originally there were 10 dwellings but in 1975 the buildings were converted to eight units by the Sawyer Partnership of architects, and the properties became administered by the Church of England Pensions Board, having previously been the responsibility of the Cathedral Dean and Chapter. Today the remit of the administrators has been enlarged to include clergy widows from the Canterbury Diocese in addition to those of Winchester and Worcester.

Just outside the west wall of the Cathedral Close, in Symonds Street, are the **Christ's Hospital Almshouses** built in 1607, and altered in the late 19th century, comprising seven dwellings in all as part of a terrace. Peter Symonds, who was born in Winchester and afterwards achieved success as a Mercer in the City of London, founded these almshouses. The purpose of the foundation was for *"the maintenance of*

Bishop Morley's College
Founded in 1672 and endowed for "The widows of ten poor clergymen of this Diocese and that of Worcester". These buildings designed and reconstructed by the architects John and John B. Colson overlook the Cathedral Green and date from 1880.

Winchester County Gaol, Jewry Street

"The Old Gaolhouse" public house today, note the similarity of the architectural details as shown in the 1832 Engraving of the then County Gaol.

Engraving of 1832 *(Authors collection)*
This picture is well related to the drawing of the ground floor
plan held in the Hampshire Record Office on the next page.

six old men, one matron, and four boys; and also for the assistance of one scholar in each of the two English Universities" namely Oxford and Cambridge. Under the terms of the will of Peter Symonds he entrusted the management and control of the charity to the Warden of Winchester College, *"for the time being"*, although today the almshouses are administered by St. John's Winchester Charity. It is recorded that in the 18th century provision was made for providing for the men, *"a gown of blue cloth, on which was to be fixed the silver badge of the hospital"*. In addition for the boys *"a coat, hat, and pair of breeches of the*

same, (i.e. blue cloth), *and a pair of leather breeches"*. A contemporary writer noted that the almsmen and boys *"exhibit the dress prevalent amongst the ordinary people of the time"*. Today the almshouses provide accommodation for five poor bachelors or widowers over 50 years of age who have lived in Winchester for over two years.

On the west side of Jewry Street are the visible remains of the **Old Gaol**, the once notorious building, now occupied in part in a new benign guise as "The Old Gaol House" public house. This prison was built in 1805 and designed by George Moneypenny and thought to be based

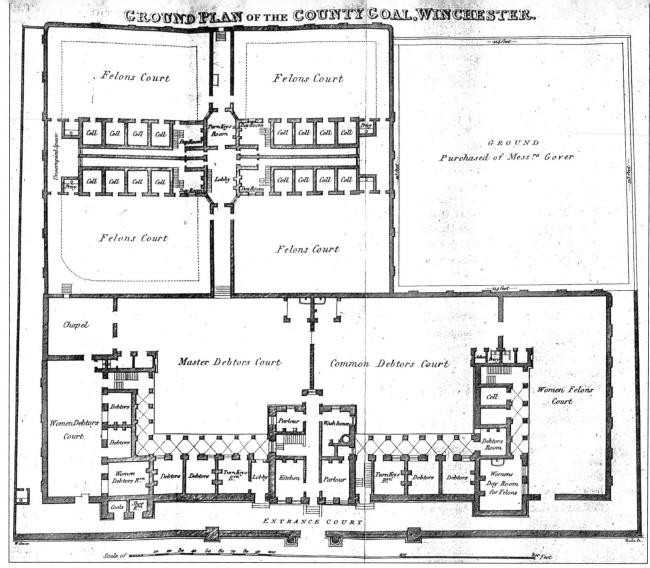

Plan of the County Gaol
Built in 1805 for the retention of both "felons and debtors".
(Published by kind permission of the Hampshire Record Office.)

on the design of Newgate Gaol in London. Although but part of the original structure remains, plans and drawings exist giving an accurate indication of its appearance and layout. Externally it was an imposing edifice as can be seen from a contemporary engraving, while the impact of the yellow brick walls and vermiculated stone quoins are today quite visible in the public house elevation and sections to the south of the same façade.

Essentially the prison catered for both debtors and what were then described as "felons" and the warders in charge were called "turnkeys". Strangely there were both "common" and "master" debtors, while immediately adjacent to both categories of debtors and felons exercise courtyards were provided which were interconnected with the prison chapel. A Dr. James Neild published a detailed narrative of the design and conditions within the prison, in March 1808, presenting a somewhat glowing report leaving an inquisitive reader wondering as to its veracity. Later, in 1817, a Committee of Enquiry confirmed only two faults; firstly that the building was too handsome in its design and advised that ideally the outside should *"present to the passing spectator in its appearance, more of terror than invitation"*. In addition it was pointed out that there was no provision for executions on site and further instructed, *"that a surveyor should make plans for a drop… in a situation that may be found more convenient for the purpose"*! Be that as it may conditions were probably no worse than considered correct at the time, and the building remained in use as the County Gaol until the new and present prison opened in Romsey Road in 1849/50.

The **H.M. Prison Winchester** is sited, as described in the introduction to this chapter, almost opposite the Royal Hampshire County Hospital, also in Romsey Road. Inside its enclosing brick walls, the main prison buildings are laid out in a "five star" configuration of "wings" around a central control area. Above this central area is the "roundel" or ventilation tower, which with its conical roof and louvres is the only feature of the main buildings easily visible outside on the main road, apart from the Gate House buildings, seen rising above a grass bank and further boundary wall.

Access to the inside of the prison compound is via the portals of the gate house, a large awesome door and smaller sub-door, which one bends down to pass through,

having first rattled the large door knocker, reminiscent of a sanctuary knocker on a medieval church! Beyond this is a small inner covered way, barred at each end, but leading beyond to the main prison wings. There are two contrasting architectural styles evident; namely the classical details of the stucco rendered facades of the gatehouse and governor's wing inside, and the brick facades and Victorian detailing of the wings housing the cells and ancillary facilities. The governor's wing running approximately north to south, is approached by a flight of stairs, and contain the administrative offices of the prison in part, (there are approximately 300 staff), and is effectively at first floor level with one floor below and two above. This floor gives access to the main floor of the prison and the four remaining radiating wings which can best be described at 8, 10, 2, and 4 o'clock positions, with the administration block and chapel at the 6 o'clock location. It is at this level also that the best view of the interior can be seen from the vantage-point of the space beneath the central roundel. The four arms of the wing stretch out with three tiers of cells facing a central corridor and at first and second floor levels the cells are reached from steel landings or balconies, with the spaces between leading to the pitched roofs above and their glazed roof-lights. At the end of each wing is an arched window feature glazed with glass bricks and although light permeates throughout the interior, and air is introduced and extracted via the "roundel", at no point is the sky visible.

A spiral steel staircase leads from the main floor of the prison to reach the chapel on the third floor, which is entered via steel and barred doors to reveal a large room distinctly Georgian in appearance, with a flat panelled ceiling and dominated by a large crucifix. This chapel is in contrast in its design to the chapel in the County

Hospital nearby which is ornate Victorian but both share the common factor of being unusually on the top floor. A full-time chaplain and others administer to the prison with services held in the main chapel for the men and in another location for the women. As a postscript to these arrangements it is stated that *"the Chaplains are always happy to speak to anyone who would like help or advice"*. This is very much in line with the current policy of "openness" in relationship to the management of the prison today. The idea of keeping the prisoners in, and the public out, has now softened to the extent that it is now possible to see inside the buildings, and with the inmates now being considered as part of the wider community rather than excluded for all time beyond the duration of their sentence. However there can be no doubting the serious purpose of prison life when for a period that most precious commodity of freedom is lost.

To the south of the Royal Hampshire County Hospital and to the west of the Peninsula Barracks, **King Alfred's College** stands on a sloping, undulating and lush green campus. King Alfred's College began as a Diocesan Training School for teachers in 1839, the brainchild of Charles Richard Sumner, Bishop of Winchester from 1827-69, who in 1838 was the driving force in establishing the Winchester Diocesan Board of Education. The first premises occupied by the training school were at 27-28 St. Swithun's Street between 1840-47, followed by a period in Wolvesey Palace between 1847-62. The college moved to its present location in 1862, when on October 13th the Bishop of Winchester opened its *"Diocesan Training College West Hill"*, in new buildings designed by the architect John Colson, and on land given by the Cathedral Dean and Chapter. An engraving of the original building, by comparison with its appearance today, shows that much

King Alfred's College
Window detail of John Colson's design for the original " Diocesan Training College".

of its architectural details have changed. However its Gothic asymmetrical design can still be appreciated, with its stone mullioned and transomed windows, and decorative brick arches set in the rugged stone walls of coursed regular rubble.

To the west of this main building is the original chapel built in 1881 and extended in 1927, and now called the

King Alfred's College
The Chapel built in 1881, (and extended in 1927), was "erected in grateful and loving memory of John S. Utterton, D.D., Bishop of Guildford", and designed in the late Decorated Gothic style.

who gave their lives in the Great War 1914-18". To the west of the main body of the chapel is a large arch marking the point where the extension was added together with the south entrance porch. In this part of the chapel is a memorial to those past students who died in the Second World War, and at the west end there are four very fine stained glass windows with one clerestorey light at the apex of the roof. Outside the architecture is distinctly Gothic in appearance and the fleche finial on the roof with its crucifix give a subliminal French flavour to its design.

In conclusion the range of buildings in this part of the city namely the prison, hospital, military barracks together with the training college, are in effect an encapsulation of Victorian society and its institutions. Nearby is the West Hill Cemetery, with its sylvan setting for all the graves, being a record and reminder of all the people who lived and died here during the great Victorian period of both Winchester's and England's history.

"Winton Chaplaincy Centre". Inside the main nave there is a beautiful braced arch timber roof, above windows with tracery in the Decorated Gothic style, with plain plaster walls, and at low level, oak wainscot panelling up to the level of the underside of the window cills. Above the wainscot is a First World War memorial in carved oak, *"To the Glory of God in Memory those Members of this College*

Statue of King Alfred
This dramatic view of the statue sculpted by Sir Hamo Thorneycroft, rising above the roof-tops of Winchester, was put in place in 1901, to mark the millennium of the end to King Alfred's reign.

Chapter 10

WINCHESTER IN THE TWENTIETH CENTURY

Winchester is symbolised by the statue of Alfred, King of the West Saxons from A.D. 871-899, when he died at the age of 50. This is a great statue to a great man, and stands proudly and defiantly in the middle of Winchester's Broadway at the end of the High Street. The statue also stands immediately adjacent to Palace Gardens, the sites of the Saxon Nunnaminster founded by Alfred's wife, and near at hand to the Mayor's official residence, Palace House. This statue was erected in 1901, the sculptor was Hamo Thornycroft, and was put in place to mark the millennium of the end of King Alfred's reign.

Returning again to the subject of the **Cathedral**, it was here between the years of 1905-12 that a great drama was enacted, when faults of such a serious nature came to light in its foundations, that this great building was almost lost, saved only by the efforts of some remarkable people. In a letter dated 5th July 1905, from the engineer Francis Fox to the Dean of Winchester, of the 12th century retrochoir, he observes that *"whereas the building has been moving for nearly 700 years, there are undoubted signs that more serious movement is taking place now"*. The reasons for this movement were summarised in the same letter namely the high water-table which had hitherto allowed the building to move with the seasons had been lowered, causing a bed of clay on which the foundation raft of beech logs rested, to dry out and shrink. The remedy suggested was to underpin the foundations and engage directly with an underlying bed of gravel some distance below the existing foundations. However there was a practical problem in that at this lower level water was present. Francis Fox was recommended to the Dean by the Cathedral architect Mr. T.G. Jackson R.A., because of the engineer's experience elsewhere where working in water was the problem. Apparently Francis Fox had been involved with such projects as the Mersey Tunnel, the London Underground Railway and Sydney Harbour Bridge.

Perhaps the most awesome feature of the whole operation was to use the services of a diver to go down into the watery darkness and to manhandle bags of concrete into position, and so rebuild the foundations step by step. The contractors chosen to carry out the repairs to the Cathedral were Messrs. John Thompson of Peterborough, and the diver was William Robert Walker. The existing foundations of the Cathedral were approximately 10 feet below ground level, and comprised layers of beech logs laid horizontally, bound together with chalk and flint, at a level below which the ground was waterlogged. Below this however were layers of clay some 6 feet deep above another layer of peat, reaching down to a firm gravel bed. Edwin Long. the Clerk of Works for the project, records that in some places, where the gravel bed was nearer the surface, timber piles had been driven into the ground to engage with the firm gravel substrata. However. it was concluded that the Norman builders, unable to deal with the waterlogged ground elsewhere,

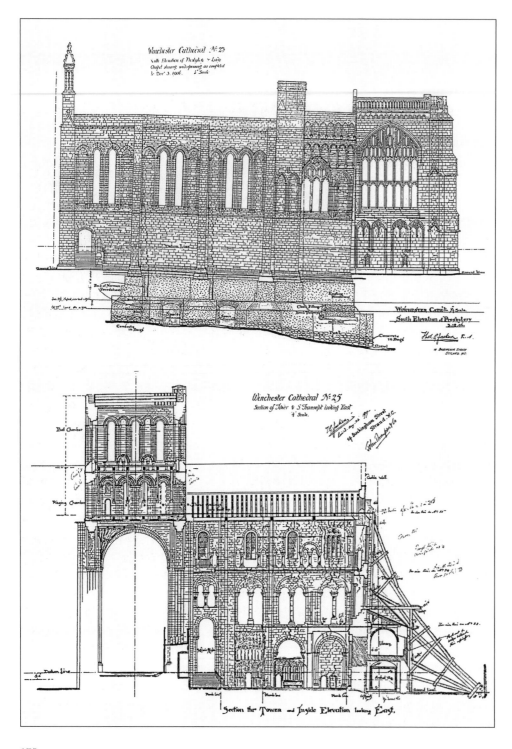

Repairs to the Cathedral and record drawings.

These two drawings by the then Cathedral architect, Sir Thomas Jackson, are held in the Cathedral archives in the Triforium Gallery in the south transept, and are beautifully executed in ink on hand-made paper.

Each drawing is a cogent reminder of the extent of the structural damage sustained within the Presbytery, and discovered in 1905.

(Reproduced by courtesy of the Cathedral Dean and Chapter.)

relied on the raft of beech logs as described. The task of the diver was, in summary; to remove the beech logs section by section and then to underpin the foundations, by inserting bags of concrete, down to the level of the gravel bed. It was this slow and dangerous task that was carried out by William Walker, backed up by a large work force at ground level.

In the Cathedral archives held in the Triforium Gallery in the south transept, are kept record drawings by the then Cathedral architect, T.G. Jackson, one showing the south elevation and Presbytery, and another a section through the tower and inside elevation looking east. Both drawings are beautifully executed in ink on handmade paper, with watercolour washes, and give a graphic indication of the damage to the superstructure, at the east end of the Cathedral, caused by the subsidence and failure of its foundations. The whole surface of the stone walls are shown both crazed and cracked, with raking shores in position to prevent the ultimate collapse. The drawing of the Presbytery shows also the alarming lack of verticality in the walls and around the windows, but thankfully there is evidence here of some of the concrete bags already having been put into position, as part of the underpinning procedure.

Both inside and outside the building additional measures were also necessary to deal with fractures in the main walls, and voids inside and out of view. In the first letter of Francis Fox to the Dean, he refers to the futility of just pointing up the cracks, without fully dealing with the fissures behind the wall face. He observes that "*a trowel cannot enter more than 2-3 inches, and this pointing, whilst reassuring to the eye, is of no value towards restoring the walls to their original strength*". It was for this reason that a method of pressure grouting was put into practice here,

Repairs to the Cathedral as carried out
This "arcade" of stone buttresses on the south side of the nave, was put in place as part of the overall repair programme of 1905-12, to stabilise the failing superstructure of the Cathedral.

whereby mortar was introduced under pressure into the holes, a procedure first learnt by Fox when working previously as consultant on the London Underground Railway system. As a result of the dual processes of both the underpinning and stabilisation of the structural damage to the superstructure, the Cathedral was saved from collapse. It was at Winchester that Francis Fox really made his name and in so doing earned a Knighthood, although without doubt the public hero of the day was William Walker, for his bravery and fortitude. A Service of Thanksgiving was held in the Cathedral on 15th July 1912, St. Swithun's Day, for a great building *"Preserved from danger by the Goodness of God"*. As an epitaph to this whole saga the words of Sir Thomas Jackson, the Cathedral architect, come to mind, *"From first to last, however, the history of the Cathedral has been marked with disaster owing to the unfortunate selection of the site"*.

One of Winchester's best known "modern" buildings is **Elizabeth 11 Court**, being part of a complex of buildings, to the north of the city's West Gate, serving as administrative offices to Hampshire County Council. Built in 1959-60 to designs by the architects C. Cowles Voysey, John Brandon-Jones, J.D. Broadbent and R. Ashton, this neo-Georgian building owes nothing to the ethos and cubism of the 1960's, and in its symmetrical plan form around an inner courtyard is reminiscent more of a classical rather than a contemporary concept. The north and south wings around the courtyard are four storeys high with dormer windows in the tiled roofs, while the east and west wings are by contrast just three storeys high. The buildings are extremely classical in their detailing and form, with some beautiful two-toned brickwork, red brick overall with "purple" bricks around the door and window openings, the latter with their traditional white painted frames and

Elizabeth 11 Court
Built in 1959-60 to the designs of C. Cowles Voysey, John Brandon-Jones, J.D. Broadbent and R. Ashton, although drawn in 1936, lay fallow for almost a quarter of a century, before it was constructed out of time and fashion.

Motisfont Court
Designed in 1995 by the
Hampshire County Architect's
Office, it is beautifully
detailed in brick and glass.
At this juncture the building
gracefully turns the corner
with some spectacular curved
glass windows.

glazing bars. Within the courtyard is a great cobbled concourse, with a circular grassed feature and planter. Massive brick piers and arches to the vaulting above mark the south entrance, while heavy granite plinths and capitals punctuate the piers, and the views through the gates, painted black with gold rosettes, of the space within, completes the picture. Outside the main entrance, and set in a small landscaped garden, is a bronze statue of a pig entitled "The Hampshire Hog", a piece of history and humour designed and made by the sculptor David Kemp in 1989.

Immediately to the north and linked to Elizabeth 11 Court, is **Ashburton Court,** built circa 1964 and designed by the County Architect and his office. These buildings are in complete contrast to Elizabeth Court, being quintessentially of a 1960's design, with the familiar use of reinforced concrete and precast panels, accompanied by glass curtain walling. Although it is now fashionable to criticise the architecture of this period on grounds of appearance, quite often such buildings are found to be successfully functional in their planning and spatial arrangements and on these counts Ashburton Court is no exception. It cleverly addresses the levels of the sloping site to give easy vehicular and pedestrian access to the two lower decks of the car park, using the roof of this element to form a podium above which the offices and glazed walkways are arranged. Although Elizabeth 11 Court was finished just four years earlier, its design took place in 1936 and lay fallow for almost a quarter of a century, before it was constructed out of time and fashion.

To the west of the main complex of the County Council offices is **Motisfont Court** designed in 1995 by the County Architect and his office. This building seeks to bridge the aesthetic gap between traditional and modern architecture. Turning the corner from the High Street into Tower Street there are asymmetrically placed gables

The Wessex Hotel
Both externally and internally this hotel is an example of good modern design. Outside the building responds to its historic setting namely the Cathedral and the surrounding churchyard, while inside the hotel is both 'plush' and restrained in its appearance and decoration.

projecting from the face of the beautifully detailed red brick walls, with ribbed sloping roofs, into which are placed elegant semicircular glass dormers. At street level the covered pavement colonnade reflects the traditional images of the "Pentice" nearby in the High Street. At the far end of the Tower Street elevation the building gracefully turns the corner again with some spectacular curved glass windows at pavement level. At the rear and to the east there is a complete change of mood and a glass wall bursts forth to greet the eyes, set behind a "trellis" of tubular steel supports surmounted by angular gables silhouetted against the sky. The brick main facades of Motisfont Court blend well with Elizabeth 11 Court opposite, but one cannot help thinking that without these contextual constraints this building would have been even more spectacular.

The **Wessex Hotel**, designed by the architects Fielden and Mawson, in association with Lionel Brett, represents an example of good modern design responding to an historic setting, namely the Cathedral and surrounding churchyard. The hotel was built in 1961-3 on a site to the north- east of the Cathedral and its "Green", in an area of land once designated as the Cathedral car park. This particular site is one of great antiquity and was the subject of significant archaeological excavations before the building took place, and the foundations of previous buildings and wells came to light thought to be of the period 1066-1119. (Photographs of these excavations are now kept in the hotel records.) The building is laid out on an "L" shaped plan, with its long arm parallel to Market Lane, and its short arm at right angles and running south on the line of Paternoster Row. The structure is essentially three storeys high, almost domestic in scale seen against the Cathedral, with a basement in which is housed the Cathedral boilers. The wing above Paternoster Row is open

The Crown (Law) Courts.
Opened in 1974 by The Lord Hailsham of Marylebone, and designed by the Louis de Soissons Partnership. This building although contemporary in its appearance, responds nevertheless to the majesty and drama of its usage and setting, being inter-linked with the medieval Great Hall, previously the scene of many great trials.

at ground-floor level to form a car park and pedestrian access to the hotel. Externally the materials are brick and flint panels at the lower level, with smooth stone ashlar panels to the two floors above. It is a well-mannered and orderly building without being obsequious. Inside the hotel is both plush and restrained in its appearance and decoration. In the main reception area there is a striking stained glass feature by the artist John Piper, seen juxtaposed with some sophisticated grained timber panelling to the front of the reception counter. Immediately past the reception is the recently renamed "Walker Restaurant", (after the Cathedral diver), with a fine view of the Cathedral, which Walker helped to save, seen across the magnificent old churchyard.

The **Crown (Law) Courts** are situated to the east of the Great Hall and are approached through some monumental steel gates designed by Antony Robinson. There is a plaque in the foyer of the Courts, stating that the building was officially opened by, "*The Lord Hailsham of Marylebone Lord High Chancellor of Great Britain on the 22nd Day of February 1974*". The architects for the project were the Louis de Soissons Partnership who produced a design in keeping with the early 1970's era, which although "contemporary" responds nevertheless to the majesty and drama of this historic site.

The approach from the High Street to the south passes the imposing bronze sculpture of "Horse and Rider", by Elizabeth Frink (1975), and pedestrians move towards the Courts via a great flight of stone steps (without thought for disabled access or so it would seem). Beyond this and to the right of the main entrance to the Courts another flight of similar stone steps moves upwards and to the west, interconnecting with the entrance to the Great Hall itself. Visually these two ranges of steps look like the sides of some great amphitheatre, and symbolise in an uncanny way the drama of the activities of the Law Courts inside.

The entrance foyer to the Courts is grand and impressive although seemingly sterile in its neutral appearance and choice of monotone materials and finishes. Once past the security check-in desk there is a grand flight of polished granite stairs leading upwards to a mezzanine level at which point it is possible to look down on the foyer and appreciate the mosaic floor below, polished marble walls, and bronze framed entrance screen. Beyond this is the vista of the outside forecourt and steps to which reference has already been made. A further carpeted staircase leads upward to the courts including Court no. 1. The approach to the public gallery of this court is via a somewhat plain, narrow and tortuous staircase. Inside the

public gallery there are tip up seats much like in a theatre, and the courtroom below is cube-like in shape with mostly blank panelled walls, apart from some high-level windows. The Judge or Recorder sits facing the court flanked by court officials in front, with the jury to his/her right, and the witness box to the left. Counsel for both prosecution and the defence face the Judge and behind sit the defendant/s. Acoustically the room works very well and every word can be clearly heard. Although the pace of the proceedings appears slow and remote there is a sense of inevitability about the outcome, deciding on innocence or guilt, and freedom or custody for those brought here for judgement.

Outside and to the south the entrance elevation presents a faceted façade of chevrons and bays, built in stone, flints, and facing bricks. There are curious little bay windows set between the chevrons at an intermediate level, reminiscent of the late 19th century office nearby in Castle Avenue. The architectural junction between the Courts and the Great Hall is visually less than perfect; far better to have used a neutral and transparent device, linking the old with the new.

The last decade of the 20th century produced three significant building schemes, namely, the Brooks Shopping Centre, the Cathedral Visitor's Centre, and the Hampshire Record Office. The Brooks Shopping Centre is sited to the north of the High Street, the traditional home of the medieval merchants, and produced on a rectangular site, a modern version of what in the 1980's was referred to as "the shopping experience". In addition, and most importantly, a major archaeological excavation preceded this development over its site, releasing much knowledge of Winchester's history from Roman times onwards. The Cathedral Visitor's Centre represents an example of a purpose-built and quintessentially modern building,

The Brooks Shopping Centre

Opened in 1991, this building complex occupies a 2.5 acre site in the centre of Winchester, whose construction uncovered important Roman and medieval discoveries, now recorded in a small permanent museum display at basement level. A detail of the tower on the north side of St. George's Street with its "carillon" or cluster of bells, ringing on the hour, harking back to the long ecclesiastical history of Winchester, when the church and commerce often shared common interests.

The Cathedral Visitors Centre
This complex of buildings, is immediately adjacent to the west end of the Cathedral but hidden from view by an enclosing an all-embracing brick wall. At the entrance there stands a carved stone plaque with the words " Winchester Cathedral Visitors Centre opened by Her Majesty the Queen on the19th November 1993." The building in the foreground is the cafeteria, an unashamedly modern structure within an historic setting.

housing a shop, cafeteria and other facilities, immediately adjacent but visually removed from the Cathedral. Winchester being a centre for both pilgrimage and tourism greatly needed this facility for visitors both to the Cathedral and the immediate environs of the Close. Finally the Hampshire Record Office is a striking landmark building both visually and because, within its vaults, there is an unparalleled record of the history of both the city and the County of Hampshire beyond.

The **Brooks Shopping Centre** was designed by BDP Architects, and occupies a site of 2.5 acres, bounded to the south by St. George's Street, Middle and Upper Brook Streets to the east and west respectively, and Friar's Gate to the north. When the centre opened in 1991 it comprised 57 units, 112,500 square feet of retail space, and parking for 360 cars underground. This rectangular building is arranged with shops on three floors around a central glazed and well-lit atrium, served by a scenic lift and staircases. Below this are two levels of parking, an unusual feature of which is a system of glazed walls looking inwards towards the atrium, leading shoppers easily from their cars to the shopping levels. It is at basement level that there is a small permanent museum display, recording the archaeological excavations which took place prior to construction of the centre, covering Roman and medieval discoveries on the site from the first century A.D. onwards. Such evidence includes the remains of a 4th century Roman town house, with its "hypocaust" or under-floor heating system. Later from the 12th century, the remains of a medieval merchant's house belonging to one Roger the vintner were found, and evidence of this, together with a reconstruction of his wine cellar is also on display. In the gloom of this subterranean room, together with both audio and the visual images, it is possible to conjure up a glimpse of Winchester's antiquity.

The Hampshire Record Office
This striking edifice, stands a stone throw from Winchester's Victorian Railway Station and in its design transcends both the old and the new. Designed by the Hampshire County Architects Office, it is without doubt the most successful of the modern buildings within the city.

Externally this building displays its structural steel tubular frame, which is seen to some effect, particularly on the St. George's Street and Middle Brook Street frontages, where these streets have been pedestrianised. Above the lower walls of stone with granite rustications, all beneath brick panels, the traditional plain tile pitched roofs provide a visual bridge between the modern and traditional images of the city. On the south side in St. George's Street there is a brick tower feature, surmounted by a steel space frame with a glazed roof enclosure, above a "carillon" or cluster of bells. These bells ring out upon the hour and recreate momentarily the ecclesiastical traditions of Winchester, not least in the use of the pyramid shaped roof structure so typical of the medieval churches

within the city walls.

The entrance to the **Cathedral "Visitor's Centre"**, is via stone steps and a ramp for the disabled, immediately next to the Close Wall on which is marked on a plaque the western extent of the Norman Cathedral. Beyond this is a further stone wall plaque on which is carved, *"Winchester Cathedral Visitors Centre opened by Her Majesty the Queen on the 19th November 1993"*. Beyond this and beneath a covered way is the Visitor's Centre shop, and within an inner courtyard is revealed, together with the completely modern cafeteria and restaurant buildings. (The latter building was added during the winter of 1998-9.) These structures, design by the Winchester practice of Plinke Leaman and Browning, are single storey, with tubular steel frames supporting in the case of the cafeteria, what can best be described as a folded "A" frame roof, with the north facing walls to the courtyard completely glazed. Inside the Cafeteria, the south facing walls are solid until the folded roof is met, at which juncture there are triangular glass inserts, following the shape of the roof above. At the east end of the main room is a curved wall, (screening the toilets), and on this wall there is a mural depicting *"medieval stained glass from the west front of the Cathedral, reconstructed in a random pattern"*. This inscription refers to the vandalism in the Cathedral by the "Roundhead" troops of Oliver Cromwell during the Civil War of 1642-6. The interior of the cafeteria is both light and airy in character, and looks out on to a paved courtyard. With tables shaded by umbrellas, all very English! The food served here includes delicious savoury toasted bread, called "trenchers", harking back to the medieval tradition of food served on square wooden plates of the same name.

The **Hampshire Record Office,** stands adjacent to Winchester's Victorian railway station and in its design transcends the old and the new. Designed by the Hampshire County Architects Office, it is without doubt the most successful of the modern buildings within the city. Sited at the junction of Sussex Street and City Road, it is a dramatic and handsome landmark building and sits comfortably upon a robust and solid substructure, above which is an elegant, light, tiered and stepped glazed superstructure, and folded "A" frame roof. In the October 1993 edition of the "Architectural Review" it states

perceptively, *"The excitement of the new Record Office is that, having announced its presence as a great strong room, it suddenly peels open....and is utterly transformed into an open and delicate series of terraces"*. Arranged on four floors with an interesting plan configuration, which changes from a rectangle at entrance level, (including an enclosed garden area), into a stepped "L" shaped plan on the levels above. For the user this is an exciting building in which to work, both on account of its architecture and the fount of knowledge within its walls. In purely planning terms this building is successful on all counts, it deals expertly with the acutely sloping levels of the site, it is easy to find, and notwithstanding its strictly urban setting is endowed with a public garden and landscaping, within its site curtilage. It is a proud and worthy building to mark the ebbing away of the 20th century, and sets a high standard and benchmark for whatever succeeds it in the 21st century.

Epilogue.

The name of King Alfred is inextricably linked with the history of Winchester, and the 20th century began with the erection of his statue in 1901 in The Broadway to commemorate his achievements of both warrior and peacemaker as well as scholar and man of god. At the end of this century his name has again come to the fore because of recent excavations to locate his last resting-place, in a most mundane location, adjacent to a modern car park in the North Walls Recreation Ground. After his death in A.D. 899 his body was first interred in the Old Minster to the immediate north of the nave of the present Cathedral. Subsequently his remains were transferred to the New Minster, outside the North Walls, on a site now called Hyde Abbey, some remains of which can be seen adjacent to St. Bartholomew's Church in King Alfred Place. However, with the dissolution of the monasteries in 1538, and again in 1787 when the same site was replaced by the Bridewell Gaol, Alfred's remains were once more disturbed. Then, in the Sunday Telegraph of 17th October 1999 a headline announced that *"The lost tomb of Alfred the Great is discovered next to a car park"*. Although the archaeological excavations would appear to have located the exact burial site and the apse of the old Abbey, further investigations will be necessary to confirm with exactitude that this was indeed the last resting-place of King Alfred, his wife Queen Aelhswith and son Edward the Elder. May they now finally rest in peace.

PETER KILBY

Prospect of Winchester from St. Giles' Hill

"The prospect of this summit was almost unlimited. In the valley beneath lay the city they had just left, its more prominent buildings showing as an isometric drawing- among them the broad cathedral tower, with its Norman windows and immense length of aisle and nave, the spires of St. Thomas's, the pinnacled tower of the College, the tower and gables of the ancient hospice, (St. Cross). Behind the city swept the rotund upland of St. Catherine's Hill; further off, landscape beyond landscape, till the horizon was lost in the radiance of the sun hanging above it"

(**Thomas Hardy** *from Tess of the D'Urbervilles published in 1891)*

BIBLIOGRAPHY

BOOKS

Andrewes Fearon, William Williams, John Foster (Editors) *The Parish Registers and Parochial Documents in the Arch Deaconry of Winchester* Winchester and London, Simpkin and Co. Ltd., 1909

Archer, Lucy Smith, Edwin *Architecture in Britain and Ireland 600 – 1500 (AD)* London, The Harville Press, 1999

Attwater, Donald *The Penguin Dictionary of Saints* Harmondsworth, Middlesex, Penguin Books Ltd., 1981

Bede, The Venerable, Translated by; Sherley-Price, Leo Revised by; Latham, R.E., Ecclesiastical History of The English People, London, Penguin Books Ltd., 1990

Biddle, Martin Wolvesey *The Old Bishop's Palace* London, English Hertitage, 1995

Blakiston, J. M. G. *Winchester Cathedral, An Anthology* Friends of Winchester Cathedral, 1970

Bussby, Frederick *Winchester Cathedral 1079 – 1979* Southampton, Paul Cave Publications, 1979

Carpenter Turner, Barbara *A History of the Royal Hampshire County Hospital* Chichester, Sussex, Phillimore & Co. Ltd., 1986

Carpenter Turner, Barbara *A History of Winchester* Chichester, Sussex, Phillimore & Co. Ltd., 1992

Carpenter Turner, Barbara *St John's Winchester Charity* Chichester, Sussex, Phillimore & Co. Ltd., 1992

Carpenter Turner, Barbara *Winchester* Southampton, Paul Cave Publications, 1980

Cave C.J.P. *The Roof Bosses of Winchester Cathedral* Friends of Winchester Cathedral, 1953

Clifton-Taylor, Alec *The Cathedrals of England* London and New York, Thames Hudson Inc., 1972

Cobbett, William *Rural Rides* London, Macdonald and Jane's, 1975

Colvin, Howard *A Biographical Dictionary of British Architects 1600 – 1840* New Haven and London, Yale University Press, 1995

Dutton, Ralph *The Age of Wren* London, B.T. Batsford Ltd., 1951

Hardy, Thomas *Tess of the D'Urbervilles* London, Macmillan London Ltd., 1978 (From Thomas Hardy Omnibus)

Henderson, Ian. T, Crook, John *The Winchester Diver - The Saving of a Great Cathedral* Crawley, Near Winchester Henderson and Stirk Ltd., 1984

Heyman, Jacques *The Stone Skeleton, Structural Engineering of Masonry Architecture* Cambridge University Press, 1999

Lloyd Woodland, W *The Story of Winchester* London, J. M. Dent & Sons Ltd., 1932

Morris, K, Hoverd, K *The Buildings of Winchester* Stroud Gloucester Alan Sutton Publishing Ltd., 1994

Mount Ray Read, D.H.Connor, Arthur. B *Highways and Byways in Hampshire* London, Macmillan and Co. Ltd., 1919

Munby, Julian (Editor) *Doomsday Book 4, Hampshire* London and Chichester, Phillimore & Co Ltd., 1982

Murray, Peter and Linda *Dictionary of Arts and Artists* Harmondsworth, Middlesex, Penguin Books Ltd., 1986

O'Dell, Noreen *The River Itchen* Southampton, Paul Cave Publications Ltd.,

Pevsner, Nikolaus and Lloyd, David *Hampshire and the Isle of Wight* Harmondsworth, Middlesex Penguin Books Inc., 1967

Roberts, Edward *In and Around Winchester* Alresford, Hampshire Laurence Oxley, 1977

Rose-Martial *A History of King Alfred's College Winchester 1840 – 1980* London and Chichester, Phillimore and Co. Ltd., 1981

Savage, Anne (translator) *The Anglo-Saxon Chronicles,* Godalming, Surrey, Coombe Books, 1996

Sawyer, Peter (Editor) *The Oxford Illustrated History of the Vikings* Oxford and New York, Oxford University Press, 1997

Shorlock, Barry *The Winchester Guide Book* An Historical Guide for Visitors Southampton, Ensign Publications

Sir Banister Fletcher *A History of Architecture on the Comparative Method* London, B.T. Batsford Ltd., 1948

Smith, R.J.L.*A Guide to Cathedrals and Greater Churches* Much Wenlock, Shropshire, R.J.L Smith & Associates, 1988

Stevenscurl, James *Oxford Dictionary Of Architecture* Oxford University Press, Oxford and New York, 1999

Sumner-Heywood *Cuckoo Hill* London and Melbourne J. M. Dent and Sons Ltd., 1987

Trollope, Anthony *The Warden* London, Oxford, University Press, 1958

Varley-Telford *Hampshire* London, A & E Black Ltd., 1909

Vesey-Fitzgerald, Brian *Winchester* London, Phoenix House Ltd., 1953

Vulliamy, Laurence *William Cobbett's Rural Rides Revisited Book* Club Associates, 1977

Warren-Thorn *Illustrated Guide to Winchester* Winchester, Warren and Son, 1902

Wing, R.G. *A short History of King Alfred's College, Winchester 1840 – 1949* Portsmouth, Winton Club

Wood, Margaret *The English Medieval House* London, Bracken Books, 1990

Woodward, B. B. *A History and Description of Winchester* Alresford Hampshire, Laurence Oxley, 1974

Wymer, Norman *The Story of Winchester* London Staples Press Limited, 1955

NEWSPAPER ARTICLES, GUIDES AND JOURNALS

Attractions in Winchester Street map with visitor locations

Church Guides
All Saints Winchester
Holy Trinity Church
Saint Lawrence-in-the- Square
Parish of St Matthew with St Paul – paper by Mr. B. Poole
Chesil Little Theatre (formerly Church of St Peter, Chesil)
St Swithun-upon-Kingsgate Church

Constructions (crucifixion) Homage to Mondrian 1966 by Barbara Hepworth Keith Walker

Copy letter 5 July 1905, *Francis Fox (engineer) to The Very Reverend Dean of Winchester* Held in Cathedral Archives

Daily Echo *"Excavations solves mystery of Alfred"* October 22, 1999

Daily Telegraph *"The lost tomb of Alfred the Great discovered next to a car park"* October 17, 1999

Hampshire Papers:

The Art and Architecture of Owen Browne Carter (1806 – 1859)

Freeman-Robin Winchester, Hampshire County Council, 1991

Henry of Blois, Bishop of Winchester a Patron of the Twelfth Century Renaissance

Riall-Nicholas Winchester, Hampshire County Council, 1994

John Colson: A Hampshire Architect of the Victorian Age Poole, Brenda Winchester, Hampshire County Council, 2000

Introducing H. M. Prison Winchester H. M. Prison Service 1999

King Alfred the Great Rodney Hoare, Crest Books, Salisbury 1991

King Alfred's College Winchester Visitors Guide

Medieval Winchester Official Guide, Winchester Museums Service 1995

Notions Winchester College